The Ultimate Roblox Game Building Cookbook

Design immersive experiences with easy-to-follow recipes for world and game development

Taylor Field-Draper

BIRMINGHAM—MUMBAI

The Ultimate Roblox Game Building Cookbook

Copyright © 2023 Packt Publishing

All rights reserved. No part of this book may be reproduced, stored in a retrieval system, or transmitted in any form or by any means, without the prior written permission of the publisher, except in the case of brief quotations embedded in critical articles or reviews.

Every effort has been made in the preparation of this book to ensure the accuracy of the information presented. However, the information contained in this book is sold without warranty, either express or implied. Neither the author, nor Packt Publishing or its dealers and distributors, will be held liable for any damages caused or alleged to have been caused directly or indirectly by this book.

Packt Publishing has endeavored to provide trademark information about all of the companies and products mentioned in this book by the appropriate use of capitals. However, Packt Publishing cannot guarantee the accuracy of this information.

Group Product Manager: Rohit Rajkumar

Publishing Product Manager: Urvi Sambhav Shah

Book Project Manager: Aishwarya Mohan

Senior Editor: Rashi Dubey

Technical Editor: K Bimala Singha

Copy Editor: Safis Editing

Proofreader: Safis Editing

Indexer: Hemangini Bari

Production Designer: Alishon Mendonca

DevRel Marketing Coordinators: Namita Velgekar and Nivedita Pandey

First published: January 2024

Production reference: 1011223

Published by Packt Publishing Ltd.

Grosvenor House

11 St Paul's Square

Birmingham

B3 1RB, UK

ISBN 978-1-80512-159-6

www.packtpub.com

Dedicated to 11-year-old Taylor and his childhood dreams of becoming a Roblox builder.

Thank you to the ones who supported his journey to make those dreams a reality, including Natasha, Ducky, and friends and family. A special thanks to my little brother Levi whom I had the honor to play many hours of Roblox with.

Shout out to the Roblox community for providing a fun and collaborative environment for those dreams to become unbounded and limitless.

I hope that this book helps you cultivate the most powerful tool at your disposal – your imagination. Happy building!

– Taylor Field-Draper

Foreword

Taylor Field-Draper, otherwise known as *Trustmeimrussian*, is a veteran Roblox developer who has made a name for himself in the Roblox community for his high-quality standard of work and unmatched devotion to his craft. With over 15 years of experience years of experience under his belt, Taylor has refined his workflow and building practices in a way that ensures his maps are highly optimized, aesthetically pleasing, and organically understood by players of all ages. Taylor's rise to popularity came in 2019 with his role in creating the *Lil Nas X Concert Experience*, after which he created many more virtual concerts and events on Roblox, ultimately playing a pivotal role in shaping the virtual event scene on the platform.

As an up-and-coming developer on the platform, Roblox Studio can be a confusing and intimidating program to use. With *The Ultimate Roblox Game Building Cookbook*, you will learn the fundamental tools and methods of building on Roblox Studio, as well as tips and tricks that will ease your development process and make your experience stand out from the rest. This book will also teach you the basics of monetizing your experience and the theory behind creating maps according to their gameplay style from the perspective of a graduate of the Roblox Accelerator Program. Developing alongside Taylor in this step-by-step process will leave you feeling prepared to create a multitude of high-caliber experiences.

During my time working with Taylor, I have come to understand how much he values sharing his expert knowledge of Roblox Studio with those who want to become developers themselves.

Taylor found building on Roblox to be a fun way to express himself during his younger years, and he anticipates that kids like him will be able to utilize their creativity in similar ways with the knowledge provided in this book.

– Natasha West, executive assistant, Microsoft

Contributors

About the author

Taylor Field-Draper is a veteran Roblox developer based in Alberta, Canada, who has been creating on the platform for over 15 years, specializing in level and game design, building, and 3D generalist work. At the time of writing this book, he works as the lead producer for special projects at Gamefam where he oversees the direction, conceptualization, and art production for some of Roblox's most popular events, particularly virtual concerts. Prior to working at Gamefam, Taylor was a freelance game developer for numerous Roblox-focused studios and dozens of games that have collectively garnered billions of accumulative visits.

About the reviewers

Deep in the metaverse, **Xeane Martinez** hailed from the Roblox platform as both a developer and a game producer. His expertise lies in game design and project management, as he had the opportunity to work with some of the heavyweights in the industry. He had the pleasure of working with and leading multiple teams in making wonderful experiences on the Roblox platform. But before he took on leadership roles, he spent countless hours refining his developer skills as a level designer, environment artist, and game designer. He is what some people might call a *Roblox veteran* as he was on the platform for well over 11 years. His dedication and passion for the platform will continue to make more projects come to life!

I thank my peers and mentors for giving me the proper guidance and motivation to do what I genuinely love, and that is making fun and exciting games! I also thank my loved ones, my mother, my father, and my partner for fully supporting me on my daunting journey in the gaming industry. I would also like to thank all the people involved in this book for making it happen; you guys are the best!

Dean Pereira is a video game developer and graphic designer, formerly working in the advertising industry, who has experience working on mobile, PC, and Roblox games as a gameplay programmer and game designer. He is skilled in C#, Lua, Unity, Roblox, Amazon Web Services, Illustrator, and Photoshop.

Table of Contents

Preface — xiii

1
Getting Started with Studio Modeling — 1

Technical requirements	2	How to do it…	10
Creating a chair	2	There's more…	12
How to do it…	2	Creating a ladder	12
Building cactuses	4	How to do it…	12
How to do it…	5	There's more…	16
There's more…	7	Making your bed	16
Creating wooden crates	7	How to do it…	16
How to do it…	7	There's more…	20
There's more…	9	Creating a stone water well	20
Building a functional TV	9	How to do it…	21

2
Introduction to Solid Modeling and CSG Tools — 25

Technical requirements	25	Unioning an arch	34
Carving out holes	26	How to do it…	34
How to do it…	26	Creating a broken wall	36
Modeling a bowl of cereal	29	How to do it…	36
How to do it…	29	From block to rock	39
Engraving details onto surfaces	31	How to do it…	39
How to do it…	31		

3

Sculpting Terrain — 41

Technical requirements — 41	How it works… — 49
Generating large biomes — 42	**Hand-sculpting hills** — 49
Getting ready — 42	How to do it… — 50
How to do it… — 42	**Creating an island in the ocean** — 52
There's more… — 43	How to do it… — 52
Creating large terrain landscapes from scratch — 43	There's more… — 54
How to do it… — 44	**Creating a desert landscape** — 55
There's more… — 46	How to do it… — 55
Stamping terrain with heightmap images — 46	**Creating a mountain with a waterfall** — 57
Getting ready — 46	Getting ready — 57
How to do it… — 46	How to do it… — 57
Modifying terrain properties — 47	**Sculpting an erupted volcano** — 61
How to do it… — 48	How to do it… — 62
	There's more… — 66

4

Learning to Use VFX — 67

Technical requirements — 67	**Flipbook particle explosion** — 77
Creating simple effects with fire, smoke, and sparkles — 68	How to do it… — 77
How to do it… — 68	**Trailing behind players** — 79
Creating hi-res fire with particles — 71	How to do it… — 79
How to do it… — 71	**Building a whirlwind** — 82
Making volumetric smoke with particles — 73	How to do it… — 82
How to do it… — 73	**Snowflakes falling from above** — 84
Beaming a laser — 75	How to do it… — 84
How to do it… — 75	

5

Building a Multiplayer Obby — 87

Technical requirements	87	How to do it…	94
Building the obby lobby	88	Creating stage 3 – Lava	95
How to do it…	88	How to do it…	95
Creating the obby template	90	Creating stage 4 – Spinning blades	96
How to do it…	91	How to do it…	96
There's more…	91	Building the winners' area	99
Creating stage 1 – Slide	92	How to do it…	99
How to do it…	92	Setting up respawn checkpoints	100
Creating stage 2 – Truss course	94	How to do it…	101

6

Designing a House — 103

Technical requirements	103	How to do it…	112
Blueprinting your house	104	There's more…	115
How to do it…	104	Adding lights and ceilings	115
Building out the walls	105	How to do it…	115
How to do it…	106	There's more…	117
There's more…	109	Creating a roof and front overhang	117
Adding windows, doors, and floors	109	How to do it…	118
How to do it…	109	Finalizing your house	119
Grayboxing the props	112	How to do it…	120

7

Single-Player Map Flow — 123

Technical requirements	124	How to do it…	124
Planning your map	124	Drawing the player forward	127

How to do it…	128	Building out the map	135
Creating a locked door	**130**	How to do it…	135
How to do it…	130	**Creating an atmosphere with lighting**	**138**
There's more…	132	How to do it…	139
Adding obstacles	**132**	There's more…	141
How to do it…	133	**Adding ambient sounds**	**141**
		How to do it…	141

8

Building a PvP Map 143

Technical requirements	**143**	How to do it…	154
Planning your layout	**144**	**Creating an outer perimeter**	**156**
Getting ready	144	How to do it…	156
How to do it…	144	**Adding volumetric lighting**	**158**
Grayboxing the map	**148**	How to do it…	158
How to do it…	148	**Finishing the map**	**160**
Risk-versus-reward spots	**152**	Getting ready	160
How to do it…	152	How to do it…	160
Placing props for cover	**154**		

9

Monetizing Your Experience 163

Technical requirements	**163**	**Private servers**	**169**
Gamepasses	**163**	How to do it…	169
How to do it…	164	There's more…	170
Developer products	**166**	**Engagement-based payouts**	**170**
How to do it…	166	How to do it…	170
Paid access	**168**		
How to do it…	168		
There's more…	169		

10
Extra Building Recipes — 173

Technical requirements	173	Building a custom emote bar	183
Modifying a weapon system	173	How to do it…	183
How to do it…	174	Enabling Team Create	186
Swords as tools	176	How to do it…	186
How to do it…	177	There's more…	187
There's more…	180	Customizing your game settings	187
Vehicle system basics	180	How to do it…	187
How to do it…	180		

Index — 189

Other Books You May Enjoy — 194

Preface

Roblox is the largest and fastest-growing platform of all time, housing a labyrinth of experiences for billions of players. It's more than a gaming platform, it's also a storefront, social hub, and building tool that empowers anyone to create fun and robust experiences that will enrapture the audience.

The Ultimate Roblox Game Building Cookbook is the perfect guide for any Roblox developer looking to take their skills to the next level. With a wide range of recipes, this cookbook covers everything from the basics of game development on the platform to advanced techniques for creating immersive experiences.

You'll learn about the best workflows for effectively using Roblox Studio and its provided tools to create custom maps, props, **visual effects** (**VFX**), lighting, and more. Additionally, you'll gain insights into designing more complex levels of gameplay, such as single-player and multi-player flows. The cookbook also covers guidance on monetizing your games and provides you with an arsenal of assets to help you every step of the way.

By the end of this book, you will have gained a comprehensive understanding of proven Roblox experience and design methods that will help you through your journey of being a top Roblox developer!

This book is broken up into three parts:

- *Building in Roblox Studio*
- *Designing Layouts*
- *Monetization and Extras*

Who this book is for

Whether you are a young Roblox player or parent, game developer, enthusiast, or educator, you will find this book an ideal tool to help navigate you through your journey of building stellar Roblox experiences.

What this book covers

Chapter 1, *Getting Started with Studio Modeling*, teaches you the basics of creating standard props and working with the primitive shapes of Roblox parts, as well as how to use plugins to speed up your workflow.

Chapter 2, *Introduction to Solid Modeling and CSG Tools*, covers the Roblox CSG tools to create unique shapes, sculpt rocks, and create shaped holes cutting through solid walls.

Chapter 3, *Sculpting Terrain*, examines the Terrain Editor and its tools, and how to use them alongside plugins to create beautiful terrain landscapes and biomes.

Chapter 4, *Learning to Use VFX*, looks at the built-in VFX options that Roblox provides, such as Particles, Beams, and Trails to create visual effects and modify their properties.

Chapter 5, *Building a Multiplayer Obby*, uses our previous knowledge to create a simple obby game with four unique stages and use spawn points to create checkpoints.

Chapter 6, *Designing a House*, goes over the workflow, starting with the planning and layout stages, of building an enterable and furnished house.

Chapter 7, *Single-Player Map Flow*, provides a complete single-player story-driven map featuring obstacles such as locked doors. We will also look at how to keep players on track and not get lost.

Chapter 8, *Building a PvP Map*, puts our skills to the test by showing us how to create a large PvP map with two team sides. We will see how to properly balance the map and scale it appropriately.

Chapter 9, *Monetizing Your Experience*, explores the different methods of how you can monetize your Roblox experience, such as through game passes and developer products.

Chapter 10, *Extra Building Recipes*, provides extra activities. We will be first customizing a weapon, sword, and vehicle system to have custom properties and attributes. We will then look at how to enable **Team Create**, followed by customizing our experience settings through the **Game Settings** panel.

To get the most out of this book

You will need to have the latest version of Roblox Studio installed. It's also best to ensure that you download the provided assets, which are linked inside each chapter's *Technical requirements* section. You can also find each of the recipes built out inside of each of the chapter asset folders to reference as you build.

Software/hardware covered in the book	OS requirements
Roblox Studio	Windows 7, Windows 8/8.1, Windows 10, or Windows 11 macOS–macOS 10.13 (High Sierra) and above

If you are using the digital version of this book, we advise you to type the code yourself or access the code via the link available in the next section. Doing so will help you avoid any potential errors related to the copying and pasting of code.

After reading this book, use the combined knowledge that you have gained to create your own experience from scratch!

Download the asset files

You can download the asset files for this book from https://packt.link/gbz/9781805121596. In case there's an update to the code, it will be updated in the existing repository of asset files.

We also have other code bundles from our rich catalog of books and videos available at https://github.com/PacktPublishing/. Check them out!

Conventions used

There are a number of text conventions used throughout this book.

`Code in text`: Indicates code words in text, database table names, folder names, filenames, file extensions, pathnames, dummy URLs, user input, and Twitter handles. Here is an example: "Rescale the part to 80, 30, 80 studs."

A block of code is set as follows:

```
game.Players.PlayerAdded:Connect(function(player)
    player.CharacterAdded:Connect(function(char)
        local trail = game.ServerStorage.Trail:Clone()
        trail.Parent = char.Head
        local attachment0 = Instance.new("Attachment",char.Head)
        attachment0.Name = "TrailAttachment0"
        local attachment1 = Instance.new("Attachment",char.HumanoidRootPart)
        attachment1.Name = "TrailAttachment1"
        trail.Attachment0 = attachment0
        trail.Attachment1 = attachment1
    end)
end)
```

Bold: Indicates a new term, an important word, or words that you see onscreen. For example, words in menus or dialog boxes appear in the text like this. Here is an example: "Select the **Fire** effect in the **Effects** drop-down menu to insert it into the part."

> Tips or important notes
> Appear like this.

Sections

In this book, you will find several headings that appear frequently (*Getting ready*, *How to do it...*, *How it works...*, *There's more...*, and *See also*).

To give clear instructions on how to complete a recipe, use these sections as follows.

Getting ready

This section tells you what to expect in the recipe and describes how to set up any software or any preliminary settings required for the recipe.

How to do it…

This section contains the steps required to follow the recipe.

How it works…

This section usually consists of a detailed explanation of what happened in the previous section.

There's more…

This section consists of additional information about the recipe in order to make you more knowledgeable about the recipe.

See also

This section provides helpful links to other useful information for the recipe.

Get in touch

Feedback from our readers is always welcome.

General feedback: If you have questions about any aspect of this book, mention the book title in the subject of your message and email us at `customercare@packtpub.com`.

Errata: Although we have taken every care to ensure the accuracy of our content, mistakes do happen. If you have found a mistake in this book, we would be grateful if you would report this to us. Please visit `www.packtpub.com/support/errata`, select your book, click on the **Errata Submission Form** link, and enter the details.

Piracy: If you come across any illegal copies of our works in any form on the Internet, we would be grateful if you would provide us with the location address or website name. Please contact us at `copyright@packt.com` with a link to the material.

If you are interested in becoming an author: If there is a topic that you have expertise in and you are interested in either writing or contributing to a book, please visit `authors.packtpub.com`.

Reviews

Please leave a review. Once you have read and used this book, why not leave a review on the site that you purchased it from? Potential readers can then see and use your unbiased opinion to make purchase decisions, we at Packt can understand what you think about our products, and our authors can see your feedback on their book. Thank you!

For more information about Packt, please visit `packtpub.com`.

Share Your Thoughts

Once you've read, we'd love to hear your thoughts! Scan the QR code below to go straight to the Amazon review page for this book and share your feedback.

`https://packt.link/r/1805121596`

Your review is important to us and the tech community and will help us make sure we're delivering excellent quality content.

Download a free PDF copy of this book

Thanks for purchasing this book!

Do you like to read on the go but are unable to carry your print books everywhere?

Is your eBook purchase not compatible with the device of your choice?

Don't worry, now with every Packt book you get a DRM-free PDF version of that book at no cost.

Read anywhere, any place, on any device. Search, copy, and paste code from your favorite technical books directly into your application.

The perks don't stop there, you can get exclusive access to discounts, newsletters, and great free content in your inbox daily

Follow these simple steps to get the benefits:

1. Scan the QR code or visit the link below

https://packt.link/free-ebook/9781805121596

2. Submit your proof of purchase
3. That's it! We'll send your free PDF and other benefits to your email directly

1
Getting Started with Studio Modeling

Roblox Studio is unique in its use of **parts**. A part is the fundamental building block in **Roblox Studio** that can be used to create literally anything in an experience. Parts can be moved, resized, and rotated. The properties of a part, such as the color and material, can also be adjusted to affect its appearance.

In this chapter, we will be manipulating parts in many ways to develop an understanding of the use of parts in creating an experience on Roblox Studio. We will be using the basic tools provided by **Roblox Studio** to create various props and assets that will be used to furnish and decorate many of the scenes we will be creating in the proceeding chapters of this book. We will learn how to use the `MaterialFlip` plugin to properly orientate textures applied to parts, and utilize a technique called **shingling** to make our assets stand out in terms of quality. Finally, we will learn about the different methods of creating ladders using parts and trusses.

The following is a list of the recipes found within this chapter:

- Creating a chair
- Building cactuses
- Creating wooden crates
- Building a functional TV
- Creating a ladder
- Making your bed
- Creating a stone water well

Technical requirements

You will need the latest version of **Roblox Studio** downloaded. In this chapter, we will be building with primitive parts, which can be found in the build kit model located inside the `Chapter 1` folder at `https://packt.link/gbz/9781805121596`.

Alternatively, you can use parts directly from the **Part** drop-down menu found in **Roblox Studio**.

Creating a chair

In this recipe, we will be creating a chair prop using primitive-shaped parts. We will start by boxing out the shape of the chair with a primitive part and then attach a *seat*, which will allow players to sit on the chair. You will see how to orientate the seat part before we apply color and wood to our chair. We will finish off this recipe by using the `MaterialFlip` plugin, which can be downloaded from here: `roblox.com/library/166951203`.

How to do it...

We will begin by creating the basic shape of the chair out of square parts. We will further render out the chair's shape by adding legs. Next, will add a seat part to the model and then detail the chair with color and the **Wood** material. To finish, we will correct the woodgrain of the chair using the `MaterialFlip` plugin.

So, to create a chair, follow these steps:

1. Insert a square part into **Workspace** by navigating to the **Model** tab in the top bar and then selecting the **Part** tab.
2. Next, select the part and then navigate to the **Property** tab. In the **Size value** field, change the increments to `2, 1.5, 2.25` studs.
3. Duplicate the square part and place it flush on top of the original part. Resize the duplicated part to `0.35, 2.5, 2.25` to make this the back of the chair.
4. Rescale the original part to `2, 0.2, 2.25`, which will be the seat of the chair. Adjust as necessary using the **Scale** and **Move** tools.
5. Next, create four legs on each corner of the bottom of the chair using a square part scaled to `0.2, 1.3, 0.2` studs.
6. Now, in the **Model** tab, select the **Rotate** tool. In the **Snap to Grid** part of the **Model** tab, checkmark the box labeled **Rotate**, and then change the number in the value field box to 5 degrees.
7. Rotate each of the legs 5 degrees outward on the *x* and *z* axes. You can see a before-and-after comparison in *Figure 1.1*:

Figure 1.1: Rotated chair legs

8. Now, to make sure there's no gap between the legs and the chair seat, select all four legs and then use the **Move** tool to move the legs upward so the tops of the legs are hidden inside of the chair part.
9. Next, insert a **Seat** object from **Toolbox** or the `Chapter 1` folder.
10. Next, place the **Seat** object onto the chair with the yellow marker facing where the player's legs will point. You can press *Ctrl + R* and *Ctrl + T* to rotate the seat or part selected:

Figure 1.2: A seat object placed on the chair

11. Change the transparency of the seat to `1` by navigating to the **Appearance** tab found within the seat's **Properties** box.
12. Change the color of the chair to (`108, 88, 75`).
13. Next, change the chair part **Material** type to **Wood**.

14. If your wood grain does not flow the proper way, select the `MaterialFlip` plugin found in the **Plugin** tab within the top bar and then click on the part with improper woodgrain to flip the texture's orientation:

Figure 1.3: Images of incorrect (left) and correct (right) woodgrain

15. Select all of the parts of the chair and then checkmark the **Anchored** box found in the **Properties** menu. This will cause the parts to remain in place and not be affected by physics.
16. With all of the parts still selected, click *Ctrl + G* to group the parts of the chair, and name the model `Chair` within the **Workspace**.

This completes this recipe for creating a chair:

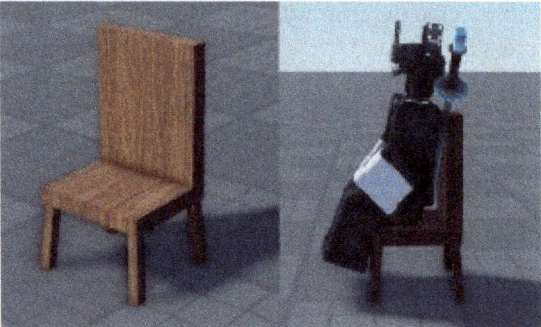

Figure 1.4: Completed chair model

You now should have a basic understanding of how to manipulate parts within **Roblox Studio**, set transparency, and use seat parts.

Building cactuses

Creating smooth yet optimal rounded ends can sometimes be a challenge on Roblox. In the following recipe, we will build a variety of cactuses through a workflow method that allows you to line up the rounded corner edges seamlessly together. We will be working with both cylindrical and spherical parts to give the cactus a proper non-blocky shape and will then learn how to rapidly create new variants of the original model. We will complete the recipe by applying differing colors and materials to give each cactus its own distinct look.

How to do it...

We will be building the body and arms out of cylinder parts. We will then then use spheres to round the elbows on the cactus arms. Finally, we will apply color and material to the model. To begin this recipe, follow these steps:

1. Start by navigating to the **Model** tab and selecting the **Part** drop-down arrow. Next, select the **Cylinder** option to insert a cylinder part onto the baseplate.
2. Rescale the cylinder part to your desired height. In this example, the cylinder part being used is 12 studs tall and 2 studs wide. This will be the body of the cactus.
3. Next, duplicate the body.
4. Rotate the duplicated part 90 degrees so that, together, both parts create a *t* shape. This creates arms for the cactus, which you can rescale to differing lengths.
5. Next, we will be creating three spheres to fit on both ends of the arms and the top of the cactus. First, we need to get the size of each sphere. To do this, select a part on the cactus and copy the number in the **Size** input box within the **Property** tab.

   For this example, the cactus body part size is 12, 2, 2, so the sphere should be scaled 2, 2, 2, as that is the proportionate size:

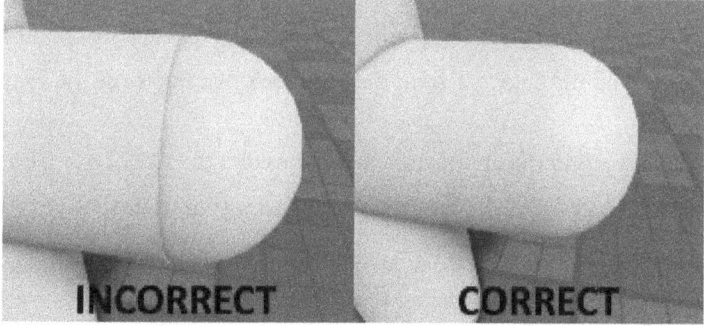

Figure 1.5: Ensure there is no crease between the ball and cylinder

6. Next, insert a sphere part and paste the dimensions that you copied in *step 5* into the sphere's **Size** box, found inside the part's **Properties** box.
7. Duplicate the sphere three times and move the added spheres to the ends of both arms and the top of the cactus, as seen in *Figure 1.6*.

   If you're having trouble placing the sphere in the center, copy the numbers in the **Position** box of the arm or body of the cactus and then paste the position number into the **Position** box of the sphere. This will center the sphere exactly in the middle of the arm or body, leaving you with something similar to *Figure 1.6*:

Figure 1.6: Finished basic model of the first cactu.

8. Now, duplicate the body of the cactus and move it along one of the arms to be flush with the spheres that we previously placed on the ends of each arm, creating a rounded elbow.

9. Next, duplicate the sphere of the arm that you just placed a cylinder part onto and move it up to round the top of the cylinder part.

10. Select all of the parts of the cactus and then anchor them.

11. With all of the parts of the cactus still selected, group them together by pressing *Ctrl + G*.

12. Next, rename your model `Cactus` from the explorer's **Workspace** or the **Properties** box of the model.

13. Now, select all the parts in the model and change the color to (`127, 142, 100`).

14. Finally, change the material of all parts to **Grass** to finish your cactus model.

This completes the final step of the recipe and should leave you with the knowledge to work with sphere parts as well as to create clean elbow bends without getting misaligned seams:

Figure 1.7: Various cactus styles

There's more...

The **Move** tool (*Ctrl + 2*) and the **Rotate** tool (*Ctrl + 4*) can be set to move or rotate in increments by typing a number into the **Rotate** and **Move** fields found under the **Snap to Grid** section of the **Model** tab. This allows for consistent placements of our parts. When doing this, it is best to move parts with increments that can be multiplied into whole numbers such as 1; for example, 0.1, 0.25, 0.5, 1. Use increments that add up to 360 when using the **Rotate** tool, such as 5, 15, 30, 90. This helps keep things aligned and scale better.

Creating wooden crates

One of the most widely used props across all genres of games is the humble **crate**. They come in many different shapes and sizes and make for a great asset that can be duplicated and stacked on top of one another. Crate models are also a prop that can be very easily scaled, stacked, and modified. In this recipe, we will be going over how to create a basic wooden crate model.

How to do it...

We will begin the recipe by creating a large cube and then creating an extruded outline along the top and bottom. Next, we will create corner and diagonal braces. To finish the recipe, we will apply color and material to the crate after we group and name the model.

Let us start:

1. Insert a square block part onto the baseplate.
2. Rescale the part to be a large cube. In this recipe, the cube size being used is scaled 5, 5, 5 studs.
3. Next, place a 0.5 x 0.5 stud block across one of the top sides of the cube. Have the part sticking out of the cube by 0.25 studs to create a lip.
4. Duplicate the top part and add it to the other three top sides. It should look like what is shown in *Figure 1.8*:

Figure 1.8: Square block outline at the top with square parts

5. Duplicate the four parts at the top and move them to 0.25 studs below the bottom of the cube.
6. Duplicate one of the side parts and then place it vertically on all four corners of the box. This completes the initial outline for the box:

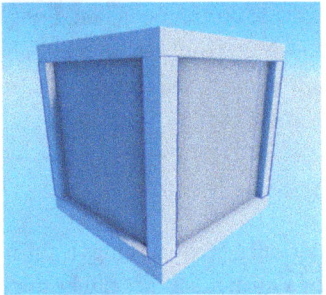

Figure 1.9: Parts placed on each corner

7. To create a diagonal part across the faces of the box, duplicate one of the vertical border parts and move it to the middle of the face.
8. Rotate the part by increments of 45 degrees until it lines up with the corners:

Figure 1.10: Diagonal brace after rotating

9. Rescale the diagonal part along its *x* axis to extend out of the other side of the box. This allows us to create the same diagonal shape on the other side of the box without using an extra part, which helps keep our total part count low, as seen in the cut-away view in *Figure 1.11*:

Figure 1.11: Diagonal brace extended onto both sides

10. Rescale the diagonal part inward `0.15` studs to give another layer of depth to the model.
11. Duplicate the diagonal part and then rotate the duplicate part `90` degrees.
12. Next, group the parts into a model.
13. Rename your model `Crate`.
14. Now, color the parts in your `Crate` model. Use a darker shade on the inside (or outside) parts of the crate so that the depth of the braces stands out better, as seen in *Figure 1.10*. In this example, I used (`108, 88, 75`) for the inside parts and (`138, 112, 96`) for the outer crate parts.
15. Finally, add material to your crate. **Wood** was the material used in this recipe's example.

    If you are using the **Wood** material, use the `MaterialFlip` plugin to fix any incorrect woodgrain flow.

That completes the recipe for building crates. Make sure to anchor your model if you have not done so already!

Figure 1.12: Finished crate

Now, you can use this model as a template to create a wide variety of crates to use across your maps.

There's more…

Z-clipping, also known as **Z-fighting**, occurs when two faces intersect with each other. This results in both materials fighting to be rendered and is often seen as flickering on the surface. To fix this, move the flickering parts up by at least `0.001`studs.

Building a functional TV

In this recipe, we will create a large flat-screen TV model that can be mounted on any flat surface. After building the TV model as a static prop, we will insert a script into the screen that will allow us to insert our own image IDs. These images will display on the TV and change every few seconds. To do so, we will learn how to modify the script to play to the parameters that we will set.

How to do it...

We will begin by scaling a square part to the size and shape of our TV and attach a wall mount to the back of it. Next, we will create a border around the TV for the screen to sit in. We will create a neon screen, and then adjust the bloom intensity of the material. To finish, we will color the TV and then insert a script, which we will customize with our own values. Let's begin:

1. To begin this recipe, insert a square part, then scale it `11, 6, 0.5` studs.
2. Add a smaller square part into the center of the back face. This part will attach to the walls so that the TV can hang.
3. Next, create a border around the edges of the TV using square parts roughly `0.75` studs thick. The border should be flush at the back and overhang the front of the TV by `0.25` studs:

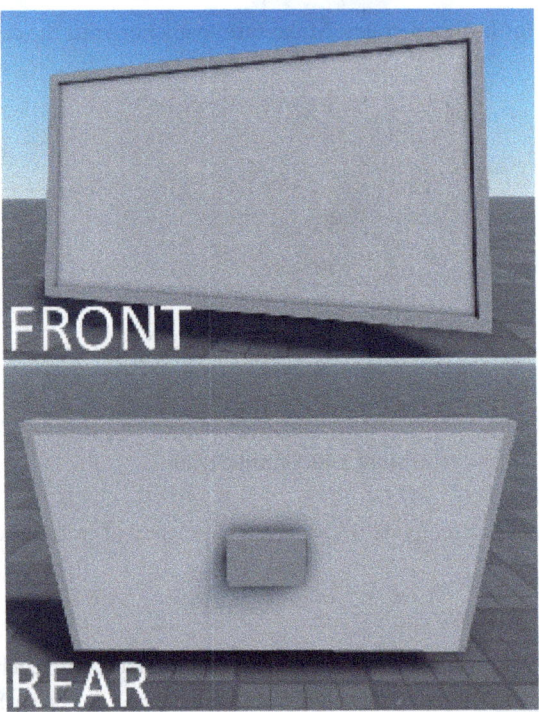

Figure 1.13: Front and back view of TV

4. Duplicate the rectangular body part of the TV and move it forward `0.1` studs to create the screen of the TV.
5. Change the material of the part we just placed to **Neon**.
6. Rename the neon screen part `Screen`.

7. Select the neon screen, open the color wheel, and select a color shade that is not overly intense, such as (159, 158, 161). You can see the difference in bloom in *Figure 1.14*:

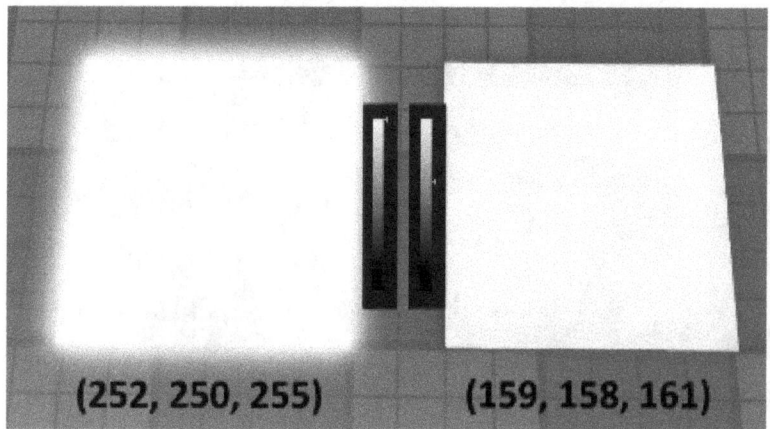

Figure 1.14: Front and back view of TV

8. Next, add two small square or cylinder neon parts to the bottom-right corner of the front of the TV. These represent the power buttons.
9. Select all the parts and group them into a model.
10. Rename your model `Prop_Tv`.
11. Now, color the parts within the TV model to (35, 35, 28).

    You now have a finished static TV prop. If you would like to add functionality to your TV, continue to *step 12*.

12. Insert into the screen part. The script is located inside the `Chapter 1` folder.
13. Double-click inside of the screen part to open **Script Editor**.
14. Paste in your own image IDs in the place of `999999`, such as `9900113573`, `13572778873`, or `13544130736`. **imageID** is a string of numbers found in the **Texture** box if you upload the image onto a decal.

    To learn how to find an image ID, check the *There's more...* section at the end of this recipe.

15. Modify the number inside the parentheses of `wait(10.0)`. The number represents the amount of time it takes to change slides. You can now exit the script.
16. Lastly, select all of the parts in the TV model and anchor them.

This completes the recipe on how to make both a static and functioning TV:

Figure 1.15: Completed functioning TV

There's more...

To find an image ID, navigate to **Roblox Studio Toolbox** and find the **Free Image search** option. Insert an image onto the face of a part, then double-click the decal to view its properties in the **Properties** menu. Copy the numbers at the end of the **Texture** link.

Creating a ladder

Roblox has a unique system that allows many different objects to function as ladders. In this recipe, we will be looking at three different methods to build a functional ladder. First, we will look at what the default truss object is and how it can be used as a climbable object. Next, we will create a rope with a part and then place an invisible truss over the top, allowing players to climb the rope. Lastly, we will use a primitive square part to build a realistic-looking and functioning ladder by using evenly spaced parts placed vertically.

How to do it...

We will first examine the truss part, which we will then use to create a climbable rope hanging from a wall. Next, we will create a ladder using blocks spaced apart vertically. Let's dive in:

1. To begin creating our first ladder, select the truss part provided in the `Chapter 1` folder.
2. Alternatively, open **Toolbox** to the **Free Models** section, search for `truss`, and then insert it onto the baseplate:

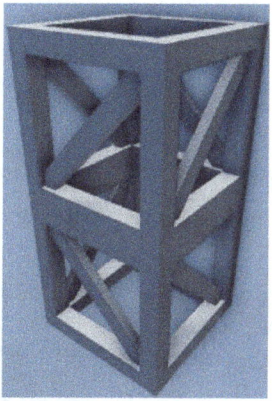

Figure 1.16: Truss part

3. Resize the truss `14` studs along the *y* axis.
4. Next, anchor the truss by checking the **Anchor** checkbox located in the truss's **Properties** box. As seen in *Figure 1.17*, you can see that players are able to climb the default truss without any modifications. This is the most basic type of Roblox ladder:

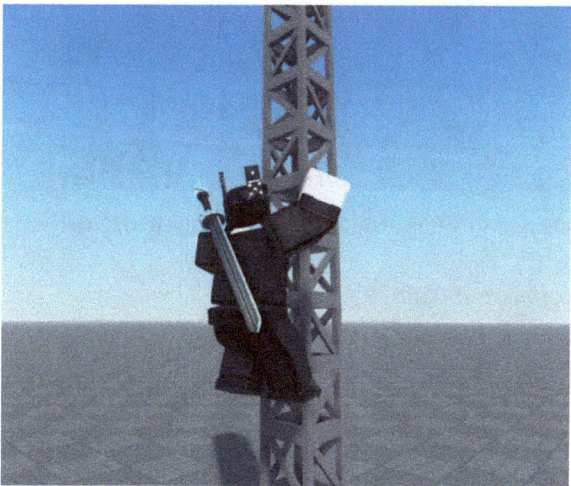

Figure 1.17: Player climbing a truss

5. To begin your second style of ladder, create a tall cylinder part the width of a rope. In this example, the cylinder is `14, 0.3, 0.2` studs and the **Orientation** value is set to `0, 0, -90`. We will be using this part to represent a rope that the players can climb up.
6. Next, create a large wall using a square part that is the same height as the rope – in this case, `14` studs tall.
7. Move the rope so that it is against the wall.

8. Now, we will create a rounded elbow like what we learned in *step 7* of the *Creating wooden crates* recipe. To do so, insert a sphere part scaled to the diameter of your rope part. Keeping the diameter of the sphere the same as the rope cylinder will help ensure that the sphere fits seamlessly into the cylinder.
9. Move the sphere along the rope until it correctly rounds the top cap.
10. Duplicate the rope part and line it up horizontally to the sphere at the top of the rope, completing the elbow, as shown in *Figure 1.18*:

Figure 1.18: Rope hanging over the edge of the wall

11. Change the rope's color to 150, 85, 85.
12. Change the rope's material to **fabric**.
13. Next, move the truss from *step 3* over the top of the rope so that the rope is inside of the truss.
14. Change the transparency of the truss to 1, making it invisible.

Now, your rope will appear to be climbable, though the player will be climbing the invisible truss inside of the rope.

15. Group the parts of the scene together and rename the model Rope. This completes the second method of creating the ladder:

Creating a ladder | 15

Figure 1.19: Player climbing the rope

16. For the third and final style of ladder, create a rectangle part. This example uses a 9.5, 1, 2 stud part.
17. Next, duplicate the part and move it up roughly 2 studs above the preceding part. Continue to repeat this step until you reach your desired ladder height. These evenly spaced parts function as ladder rungs, which enables players to climb them like a ladder.
18. Now, place vertical ends on both sides of the ladder using two square parts. Rescale the part just beyond the top of the ladder rungs.
19. Select every other rung part on the ladder.
20. Now, change the part color of the selected rungs to a slightly darker color tone than the other rungs. In this example, the lighter rungs are colored (99, 95, 98) and the darker rungs are colored (77, 74, 76). This creates a contrast in the colors by alternating the lighter and darker tones.

This completes the third method of creating ladders as well as this recipe:

Figure 1.20: Player climbing a ladder made of square parts

You now have the understanding to create a variety of climbable surfaces.

There's more…

Trusses can only be scaled in increments of 2 studs at a time. They have a minimum size of 2 x 2 x 2 and a maximum size of 64 studs.

Making your bed

Making your bed tends to be a daily task in real life. On Roblox, thankfully, you only need to make it once. In this recipe, we will be using the building tools within **Roblox Studio** in combination with primitive parts to create a bed template, and then detail it with a headboard and bed frame legs. We will then create blankets and pillows. We will complete this recipe by finalizing the bed with color and a material.

How to do it…

In this recipe, we will first build the bed's frame out of different-shaped parts. We will then create a mattress and pillows, followed by covering the bed with sheets. We will finish by draping the sheet over the edges of the bed at the bottom of the bed.

Let's look at how we can do this:

1. To begin, insert a square block part onto the baseplate.
2. Next, rescale the part to roughly the size of a bed. In this example, we will be scaling the part to 10, 1.25, 14 studs:

Figure 1.21: Legs attached under the bed frame

3. Now, to make room to place the legs, move the part up 0.75 studs from the baseplate so that the bed is levitating above the baseplate:

Figure 1.22: Bed leg moved inward from the corner

4. Now, using square parts, create four bed legs, one under each corner of the bed. The legs used in this example are scaled 0.5, 0.75, 0.5 studs.
5. Move each of the table legs inward 0.15 studs from the tabletop's edges to add depth to the model.
6. Next, create a headboard along the back end of the bed using a square part.
7. Next, insert a wedge part, place it on one of the sides at the top of the headboard, and rescale it to be roughly half of the length of the headrest. In this example, I have the wedge sloping inward.
8. Duplicate the headboard wedge part and rotate it 180 degrees, then place it on the opposite side of the headboard, as seen in *Figure 1.23*:

Figure 1.23: Wedges on headboard

9. Duplicate the original part sitting on top of the legs and then move it to sit on top to create the mattress.
10. Now, to help tell the pieces apart, change the mattress part color to `Pearl (231, 231, 236)`.
11. Using a cylinder part, round the end of the mattress at the bottom end of the bed opposite to the headboard, as seen here:

Figure 1.24: Breakdown photo of the parts used to round a mattress

12. Now, insert a square part and rescale it to the shape of a pillow. In this example, the pillow is `3.5, 1, 2` studs.
13. Using four individual cylinder parts, place them on each corner of the pillow to round the edges.
14. Next, duplicate the pillow's square body parts.
15. Rescale the duplicated part to fill the gap between the corners, as shown in *Figure 1.25*:

Figure 1.25: Breakdown photo of the parts used to round a pillow

16. Group the parts of the pillow and name the model `Pillow`.

17. Now, recolor the parts within the pillow group to (231, 231, 236).
18. Move the pillow onto the bed below the headrest.
19. Now, rotate the pillow so that it's leaning against the headrest.
20. Next, duplicate the pillow and move it beside the first to finish the pillows.
21. To create a bed sheet, duplicate the mattress and rescale it to sit over the top of the mattress by 0.15 studs on all 6 sides.
22. Rescale the top of the bedsheet (the end where the pillows are) back 2 studs so that the mattress is visible.
23. Now, duplicate the sheet part and create a second bedsheet at the foot of the mattress. In this example, the foot sheet is scaled to 10.2, 1.65, 2.3, as shown here in *Figure 1.26*:

Figure 1.26: Foot sheet

24. Now, color your bed sheets and frame. In this example, the color for the sheets is 236, 57, 57 and the color of the bed frame is 165, 126, 107.
25. Next, add the **Wood** material to the bed frame and legs.
26. Select all the parts and group them, then rename your model Bed.

This concludes the final step of creating a bed model. If your bed falls apart when you test the place, it means that you probably didn't anchor your parts! Make sure to remember that as you build through each recipe in this cookbook:

Figure 1.27: Completed bed model

You now should have an understanding of the ways to overlay parts onto each other as well as how to use the seat part as a method of letting players lay on the bed (see the *There's more...* section at the end of this recipe).

There's more...

Remember using the seat part for the chair in *step 7* of the *Building cactuses* recipe? Well, if you use the same seat part but have it rotated at an angle on top of the bed, players can then lay on the bed:

Figure 1.28: Player lying on the bed, or are they sitting?

Creating a stone water well

In this recipe, we will go over the process of creating a stone water well. We will create a circular shape out of stone bricks with a hollow center. We will then build a sloped, shingle roof over the top of the well with a shingle pattern created with randomly sized and offset parts. Next, we will cut out a part of the ground using the **CSG** tool, but we will do so in a way that does not break the hole's collisions. To finish the well, we will create stone walls that lead to a pool of water at the bottom of the well.

How to do it…

We will begin by creating a circle of bricks. Then, we will copy and stack the bricks into layers until the well is three layers high. Next, we will create a frame for the roof to attach to and use wedges to get our roof's slope. We will then cut a hole into the ground and put water at the bottom. To finish this recipe, we will shingle the roof in an organic manner.

Let's look at how we can do this:

1. Start by inserting a part and shaping it into a rectangular brick for the well. This example's brick is scaled `3.5, 1.5, 0.5` studs.
2. Duplicate the part and move the duplicated part forward around 8 studs.
3. Select both parts and duplicate them.
4. With both parts selected, rotate them `60` degrees. Repeat this process until you have a circle of bricks. If you are having trouble with where your **Rotate** or **Move** tool arrow selectors are pointing, you can switch to **Global** and **Local** movements by using *Ctrl + L*:

Figure 1.29: Circle of bricks

If the brick edges are intersecting, you may need to reduce the length of your brick.

5. Select all the parts, group them, and then rename the model `BrickLayer`.
6. Select the model, then copy (*Ctrl + C*) and paste (*Ctrl + V*) on top of the first brick layer or duplicate the group and move it up manually.
7. Next, rotate the top layer of bricks `30` degrees.
8. Create two poles symmetrically on both sides of the well with either square or cylinder parts. The poles in this example are `0.5, 9.5, 1` studs tall:

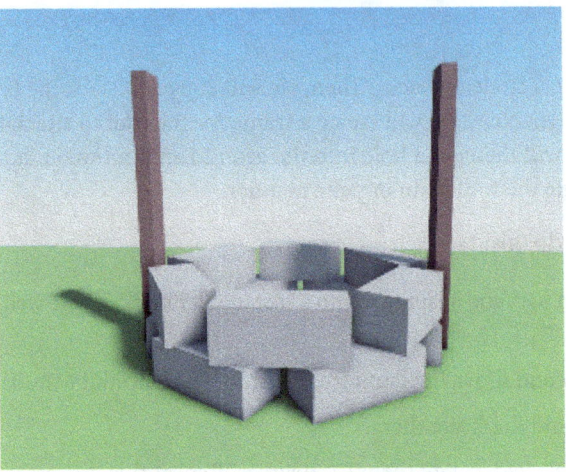

Figure 1.30: Tall pillars for the roof

9. Place two same-sized wedges connecting the roof from one pole to the other.
10. Place a part onto the sloped face of one of the wedges, then rescale it to fit the surface. Duplicate the part and place it on the other wedge.
11. Next, rescale both of the parts that we placed in *step 10* so that they overhang the wedge by around 4 studs and overhang the bottom of the wedge by 1 stud. It should look like what's shown in *Figure 1.31*:

Figure 1.31: Roof overhanging the well

12. Delete both wedges.
13. Lower the two sloped roof parts downward so that they are merged into the posts such that the roof is not levitating above the posts.

14. Insert a cylinder brick and resize it to fit the inside of the well.
15. Color the cylinder brick (`13, 105, 172`) to represent water.
16. Duplicate the cylinder part and then rescale it to be both above and below the baseplate part.
17. Negate the cylinder part by pressing *Ctrl + Shift + N*.
18. Select both the baseplate and the negated part and unite them with *Ctrl + Shift + G* to create a hole in the ground.
19. Move the blue water part to the bottom of the hole.
20. Change the water part transparency to `0.6`.
21. Duplicate the water part three times, each time moving the part `0.75` studs above the last to create multiple layers of water.
22. Now, use a cylinder part to create a beam between the two parts holding up the roof. Rescale the cylinder part to fit in between the two poles underneath the roof. The beam size in this example is `9.9, 0.5, 0.5`:

Figure 1.32: Row of shingles

23. Insert a cylinder part and place it vertically on top of the beam that we made in *step 22*. This will be a rope leading into the well.
24. Rescale the rope part to be `0.3 x 0.3` studs in width.
25. Next, recolor the rope cylinder to (`27, 42, 53`).
26. Now, create a thinner rope leading from the rope on the beam to the bottom of the well.
27. Select the rope parts and turn their collisions off by unchecking the **CanCollide** box in the **Properties** box. This will cause players to pass through the rope and not get stuck on it.
28. Now, to create shingles, start by creating a row of varying sizes of parts along one of the sides of the roof.
29. Rotate the bricks so that they peel upward at varying angles.

30. Duplicate the row and then reposition the shingles along the rest of the roof in a staggered fashion.
31. Group all the shingles on one side of the roof and then duplicate the group to the other side. Make sure to randomize the shingles on the other sides so that they don't simply look mirrored.
32. Color all the roof shingles (`190, 104, 98`).
33. Select random singles and slightly raise or lower the color shade to give the roof a stylized look.
34. Insert a square part along the top gap of the well's roof and scale it to extend over both sides of the well by about `0.5` studs.
35. Finish coloring the well by making the pillars and roof base (`86, 66, 54`) and the stone rocks on the well (`99, 95, 98`).
36. Materialize your well by applying the **Wood** material to the brown-colored parts and applying the **Slate** material to the shingles.

This completes this recipe:

Figure 1.33: Completed well model

You now have a basic understanding of the **Union** tool, as well as how to create a single pattern that can be used in many different cases.

Now, after completing the recipes found in this first chapter of this cookbook, you should have a decent grasp of the different tools, as well as some of the use cases that plugins have while building your maps and models. With a good grasp of how to build with primitive parts, let's move on to the next chapter for a more in-depth look at solid modeling and the necessary CSG tools.

2
Introduction to Solid Modeling and CSG Tools

Roblox Studio offers a set of tools that allow you to join or subtract two or more primitive parts, thus creating a variety of unique shapes that otherwise would not be possible. This chapter will outline the four different operations that can be done with solid modeling (also known as **Constructive Solid Geometry** (**CSG**)) tools, including **Union**, **Intersect**, and **Negate**, as well as the **Separate** operation. By the end of this chapter, you will have a very solid understanding of solid modeling (no pun intended).

Through this chapter, we will go through the following recipes:

- Carving out holes
- Modeling a bowl of cereal
- Engraving details onto surfaces
- Unioning an arch
- Creating a broken wall
- From block to rock

Technical requirements

You will need to open the latest version of Roblox Studio on a blank baseplate. Optionally, you can also download the needed plugins here:

- www.roblox.com/library/166951203
- www.roblox.com/library/165534573

Carving out holes

One of the best use cases for solid modeling tools is that they provide you with the ability to quickly cut shapes and holes in any primitive part. To demonstrate this, we will create a sink with a faucet. However, rather than building around the sink extruded into the countertop, we will use the **Negate** and **Union** functions to cut a hole that is the shape and size of our sink.

How to do it…

We will begin by creating a simple sink cabinet and countertop using square parts. Then, we will create the shape of the sink and **Negate** a slightly smaller part inside of the sink, allowing us to create a hollow sink once we **Union** the two parts together. We will then position the sink, and use another negated part to create a pocket for the sink to sit in on the counter. We will then finish off by building a faucet. To do so, follow these steps:

1. Insert a square part on top of the baseplate.
2. Rescale the part to be the size of your desired cabinet, which we will later attach a sink to. In this example, my part is 3, 2.5, and 3 studs.
3. Duplicate the part and move it on top of the first.
4. Rescale the duplicated part down to the height of a countertop, about 0.35 studs tall.
5. Now, rescale the countertop so that it's overhanging the cabinet on each side by 0.25 studs, as shown here:

Figure 2.1: The top part overhanging the cabinet body

6. Add two square parts to the front of the cabinet, about 0.1 studs thick. Leave a small gap down the middle, as shown in *Figure 2.2*:

Figure 2.2: The sink cabinet

7. Next, add a square part on top of the countertop and rescale it to the desired size of your sink. In this example, my sink part is 2.5, 1, and 1.7 studs.
8. Duplicate the sink part.
9. Now, rescale the duplicated part inward by 0.1 studs on every side but the top.
10. Extrude the duplicated part out the top so that it sticks out the top of the sink by about a stud.
11. Now, negate the duplicated sink part by using *Ctrl + Shift + N*.
12. Select both the negated and the original sink part and union the two parts together by using *Ctrl + Shift + G*. This will cut a hole that is the shape of our sink into the cabinet and countertop.

Figure 2.3: The sink positioned

13. Now, create another part that fills the inside volume of the sink.
14. Move both the sink part and the sink filler part down so that they only extrude the countertop by about 0.1 studs.
15. Select the sink filler part and negate it.
16. Duplicate the negated part.

17. Select one of the negated parts and the countertop, and union them together.
18. Now, select the other negated part and the cabinet part, and union them together. You should now have a hole created in both the countertop and the cabinet, which allows your sink to sit undisturbed:

Figure 2.4: The sink seated inside the cabinet

19. Create a tap and faucet for the sink.
20. Create a drain plug using a cylindrical part, and place it at the bottom of the sink.
21. Using square parts, create door handles on the front of the cabinet doors.
22. Change the cabinet body to the **Wood** material.
23. Select all of the parts and anchor them.
24. Lastly, adjust the color of the sink parts. To change the colors of a unioned part, the **Use Part Color** checkbox must be selected inside of the **Unions** property box. The colors used in this example are as follows:

   - Cabinet: 165, 123, and 81
   - Sink: 199, 199, and 199
   - Door handles: 165, 158, and 65
   - Hot water tap: 199, 53, and 27
   - Cold water tap: 41, 76, and 199

You now have a completed sink model, which you created mainly by only using a few large parts that you hollowed out, in order to create the shape and make everything fit tight:

Figure 2.5: The completed sink model

With our new understanding of how unioning negated parts works, let's move on to the next recipe, which follows a similar route.

Modeling a bowl of cereal

Smooth modeling tools are very useful for creating intricate shapes that would otherwise not be possible to make with regular primitive parts. In the following recipe, we will examine how to efficiently turn a sphere part into a bowl, and then we will use cylinder parts to fill the bowl with milk and create our pieces of cereal to fill the bowl with.

How to do it...

We will first create the bowl by negating a slightly smaller sphere inside of itself and using a square negated part, running through the middle of the sphere, to cut open the top, giving us the shape of our bowl. Then, we will place a cylindrical part representing the milk inside the bowl, scaling it to fit, and then we will create looped bits of cereal to fill the bowl with. To do this, follow these steps:

1. Insert a sphere part onto the baseplate where you want to build your bowl.
2. Rescale the sphere to make it larger and easier to work with, to a size such as 14, 14, and 14 studs.
3. Next, duplicate the sphere part.
4. Rescale the sphere part to shrink it by 1 stud equally along all sides. You can do this by holding *Ctrl* as you rescale.
5. Negate the inside sphere by using *Ctrl* + *Shift* + *N* or through the **Solid Modelling** section of the **Model** tab.
6. Select both spheres and union them together, in order to hollow out the center of the bigger sphere.

7. Now, place a large square through the halfway point of the sphere, and rescale the part so that the square part intersects through the top half of the sphere, as shown in *Figure 2.6*:

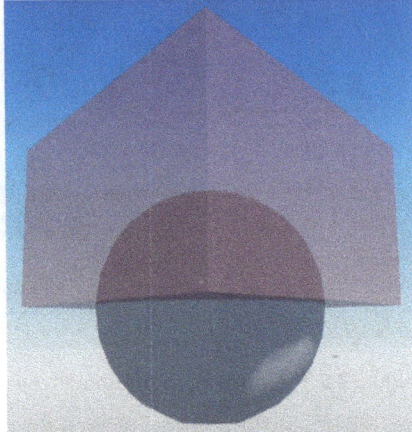

Figure 2.6: The part intersecting the top half of the sphere

8. Negate the square part.
9. Select both the sphere and the negated part.
10. Union both parts together to cut the bowl in half.
11. Next, insert a flat cylindrical part inside of the bowl to represent the milk.
12. Insert another cylindrical part, and scale it to be roughly `0.5`, `3`, and `3` studs. This will be a piece of cereal.
13. Duplicate the cylindrical part, and then rescale it to be `2`, `1.5`, and `1.5` studs. It should be centered on the original part and extruding from the top and bottom.
14. Now, negate the smaller cylinder part.
15. Select both cylinder parts and union them together.
16. Select the union part, and then enable **UsePartColor** within the property box.
17. Change the color of the cereal piece to `199`, `167`, and `134`.
18. Now, move the piece of cereal inside of the bowl.
19. Duplicate the cereal, and reorientate it so each piece looks to be floating uniquely, not just copied and pasted around. Continue this step until you're satisfied with the milk-to-cereal ratio.
20. Select all the parts and group them together.
21. With all of the parts still selected, anchor the parts.
22. Rename the model `BowlOfCereal`.
23. Rescale the model to a more realistic size.

You now have a bowl of cereal ready to be served!

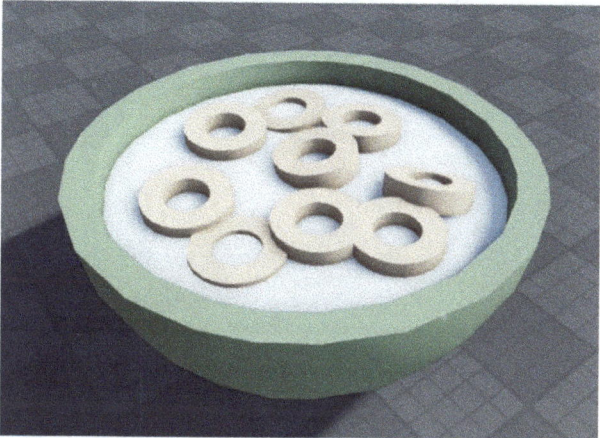

Figure 2.7: The completed bowl of cereal

You now have a firm grasp on how you can use negate and union CSG tools to manipulate any shape, whether it be a square, cylinder, or circle. Let's now dive a bit deeper into how you can use the same tools to carve fine details across various surfaces.

Engraving details onto surfaces

Detailing can be tricky, especially when you're trying to engrave small details across a large area of parts. In this recipe, we will examine the step-by-step method to accurately transcribe details and even carve out a whole cylindrical set of stairs, leading from the center of what was a square block. By the end of this recipe, you will be left with a deeper understanding of how you can use the smooth surface modeling tools to heighten the level of detail in your builds.

How to do it...

We will first insert and rescale a square part to our desired size. Next, we will stack cylinders on top of one another, making the one above 2 studs wider than the one below it. After negating the cylinders and unioning them to the square base, we will create a border and details on the top surface of the platform. Lastly, we will move the detail pieces down until they extrude into the ground part, so when we negate and union the cylinders to the square part, we will be left with an ingrained pattern. To do this, follow these steps:

1. Insert a square part into the Workspace on the baseplate.
2. Rescale the square part as 50, 5, and 50 studs.
3. Next, insert a cylindrical part in the middle of the square base.

4. Rescale the cylindrical part as 1, 33, and 33 studs, as shown here:

Figure 2.8: The scaled cylinder part

5. Copy and paste the cylinder on top of the original.
6. Rescale to enlarge the top cylinder part by 1 stud on the *Y* and *Z* axes.
7. Copy and paste the larger cylinder part, place it on top of the previous cylinder, and then move it down 0.05 studs.
8. Enlarge the new top cylinder part by 1 stud on the *X* and *Z* axis so it extends over the previous cylinder part, and then move it down 0.05 studs. You should now have a reverse stack of stairs, as shown in *Figure 2.9*:

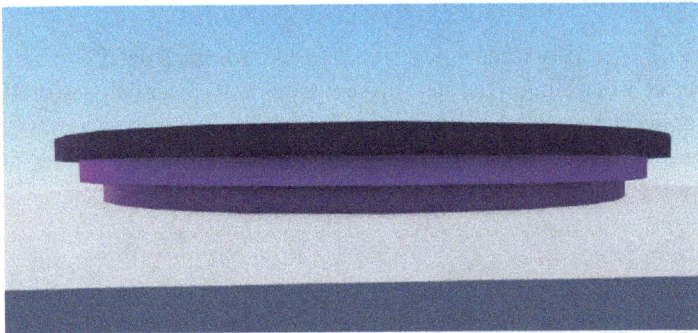

Figure 2.9: A reverse stack of stairs

9. Select the three cylinder parts and union them together.
10. Next, negate the union.
11. Move the three negated parts down until only 0.05 studs of the top cylinder are left extruded from the square block part.
12. Select the square part from *step 1*, along with the three negated cylinders, and union them all together. This should leave you with circular steps cut into the center of the square block:

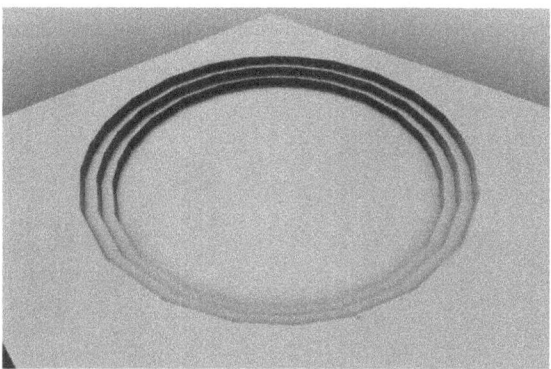

Figure 2.10: Steps unioned into the square block

13. Place square parts that are roughly 1 stud wide and 0.5 studs thick around the top face perimeter of the square, creating a border, as shown here:

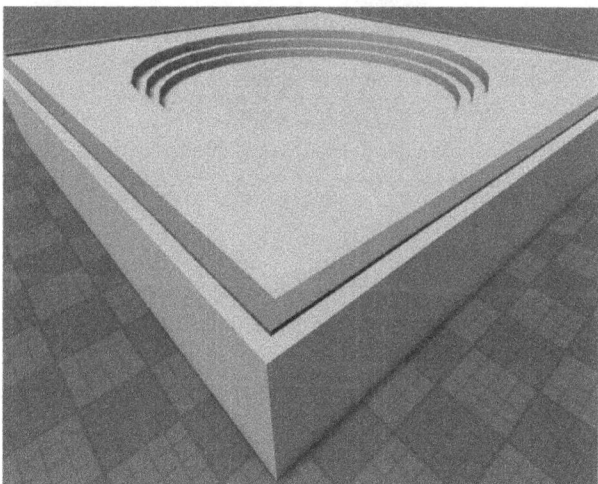

Figure 2.11: Steps unioned into the square block

14. Move the four border parts inward 0.75 studs from the outer edge.
15. Continue to place more details on the top surface of the square block.
16. Next, select all the border and detail parts, and union them together.
17. Move the newly unioned parts down 0.4 studs so that the union only extrudes from the top of the square part by 0.1 studs.
18. Negate the union.
19. Now, select the square stair union and the negated union, and union them both together. This will leave you with engravements along the top of the square stairs part.

You have now completed this recipe, and this is how the finished stair platform should appear:

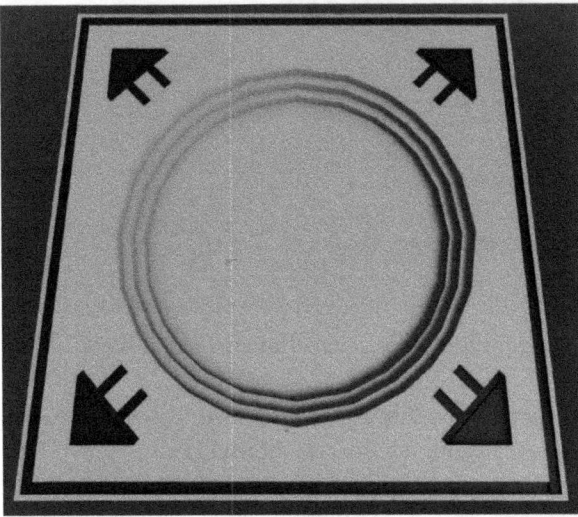

Figure 2.12: The finished engraved stair platform

You now have a method to create unique details, extruded into parts using the **Negate** function.

Unioning an arch

A great way to speed up your building and solid modeling process is to build the shape that you want to cut out separately from the part that you're cutting from. This recipe will demonstrate a way of mastering this technique by first building a wall, and then building the arched shape of the separate entrance. We will then use the **Negate** and **Union** functions to carve our desired shape. Let's see how we can do so next.

How to do it...

We will create a flat wall and then create the shape of the arch entrance using a square and cylinder part, rescaling the parts to extend them through both sides of the wall. Then, we will negate the entrance parts and union them into the wall, giving us our arch. To do so, follow these steps:

1. Begin by inserting a square block part into the baseplate.
2. Rescale the square part to be roughly 27, 34.5, and 3.75 studs. This will be the wall that we will cut the archway into.
3. Next, duplicate the wall part.
4. Rescale the duplicate to set a scale of 18, 22, and 5. Move the rescaled part down so that it sits on the ground. This will be the first part of the archway:

Unioning an arch

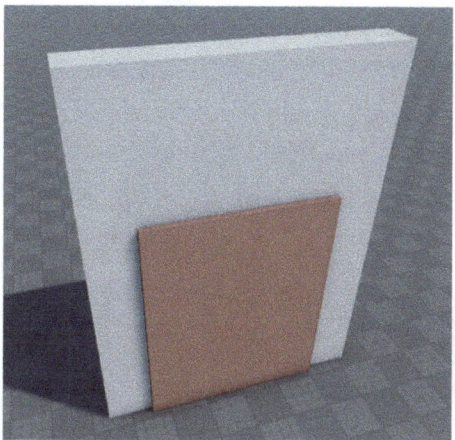

Figure 2.13: The part for the archway

5. Insert a cylinder part.
6. Rescale the cylinder part to 5, 19, 18 studs.
7. Place the cylinder part on top of the first part of the archway.
8. Now, move the cylinder part down about 9 studs or until it's flush at both ends with the square archway part, as shown in *Figure 2.14*:

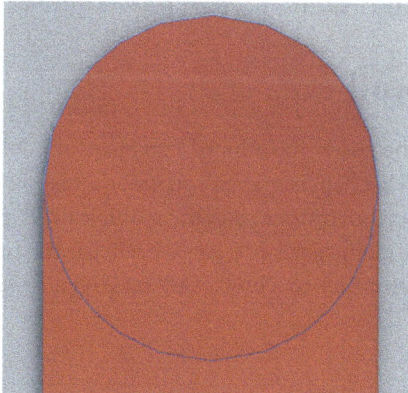

Figure 2.14: The properly flushed cylinder on the square brick

9. Now, select both the square and cylinder archway parts and ensure that they both extrude out both sides of the wall. This is to ensure that we cut fully through the wall when we union later.
10. Negate both parts.
11. Select the wall and both negated parts.
12. Union the three parts together.

The result from this should be a clean and symmetrical archway cutout in the wall, concluding this recipe:

Figure 2.15: The finished archway

You now know a quick and easy way to create arched entryways. Let's now look at how we can utilize the CSG tool that we have yet to discuss – the intersect tool.

Creating a broken wall

In this recipe, we will examine the newly introduced **Intersection** tool, now available in the latest version of Roblox Studio. Unlike what happens when you union a negated part, where it cuts the shape out of the other block, the intersect tool instead takes the multiple overlapping parts and produces the shape of the inside volume, where all the parts overlap. We will use the **Intersection** tool to create the shape of a hole, which we will then attach to a brick wall, making it appear old or damaged.

How to do it...

After building a wall, we will add a top cap as well as side pillars to help define the wall. We will then create the shape of the hole on the front face of the wall and union the parts of the hole together. We will then duplicate both the wall and hole part, so we can use the intersect tool to create a solid hole piece. Then, we will duplicate the newly created hole piece so that we can negate and union it to the original wall, creating a hole that we will fit in place of the gaping hole in the wall. To do so, follow these steps:

1. Start by inserting a square part into the baseplate.
2. Next, rescale the part to be the size of a large wall. In this example, the wall part size is `59`, `34.5`, and `3.75` studs.

3. Copy and paste the wall on top of itself.
4. Rescale the top wall part down to be roughly `1` stud tall. This will be the wall cap.
5. Rescale the top wall cap so that it overhangs each of the four sides of the wall by `0.5` studs.
6. Next, add a thick square pillar on both ends of the wall. The part sizes used in this example are `2.25`, `36.5`, and `6.25` studs.
7. Darken the shade of color of the pillars and top wall cap to help differentiate it from the main wall. In this example, the color is `147`, `146`, and `149`.
8. Next, using square and wedge parts, create the shape of a hole in the wall:

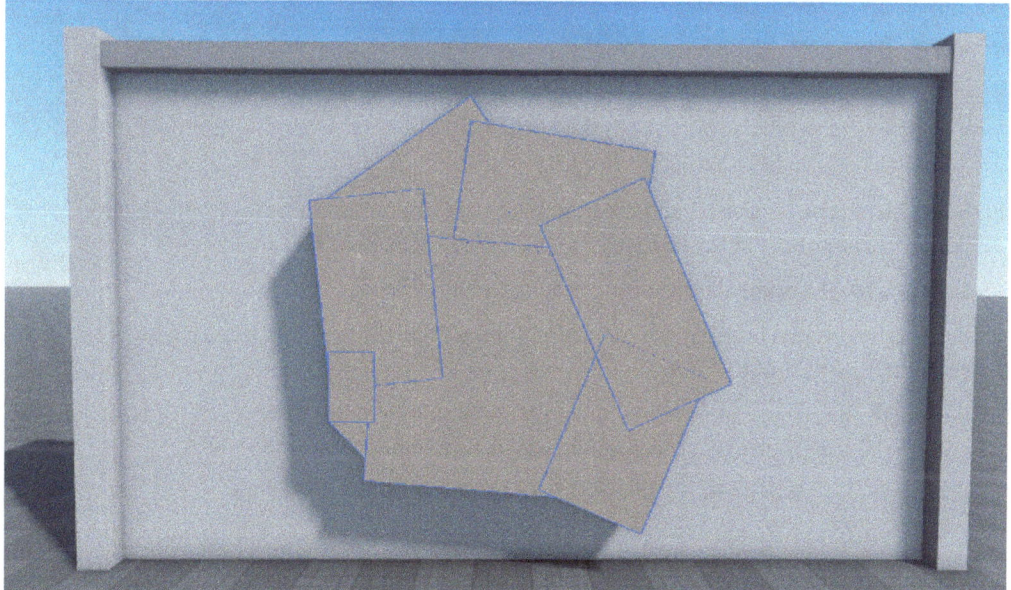

Figure 2.16: The hole shape created along the face of the wall

9. Select all the parts used to create the hole shape, and rescale each of them to stick out both ends of the wall.
10. Now, union the hole-shaped parts together.
11. Select the main wall part and then duplicate it.
12. Move the duplicated main wall part back `15` studs on the baseplate.
13. Next, move the hole shape union back `15` studs as well.
14. Select the duplicated main wall part and the hole shape and then intersect them together by using *Ctrl* + *Shift* + *I*. This will leave you with a solid shape of just the hole:

Figure 2.17: The intersected hole

15. Duplicate the hole part.
16. Move the duplicated hole part back up 15 studs, and then rescale it so that it extrudes out of both sides of the wall.
17. Negate the duplicated hole part.
18. Select the negated hole part and the main wall part, and union them together. This will leave you with a large hole in the wall.
19. Now, change the original hole intersection material to **Brick**.
20. Return the original hole piece intersection forward 15 studs so that it fits inside of the hole cutout that we just made in *step 17*.
21. Rescale the hole piece intersection inward on both sides of the wall by 0.25 studs, helping to give off the appearance that the concrete wall is just a thin layer on the wall.
22. Finally, anchor all of the parts.

And with that, we have completed yet another recipe. Through creating this broken brick wall, we learned how to use the **Intersection** CSG tool to create a perfect shape of the hole, which we then used to cut out the necessary shape that we needed in the wall:

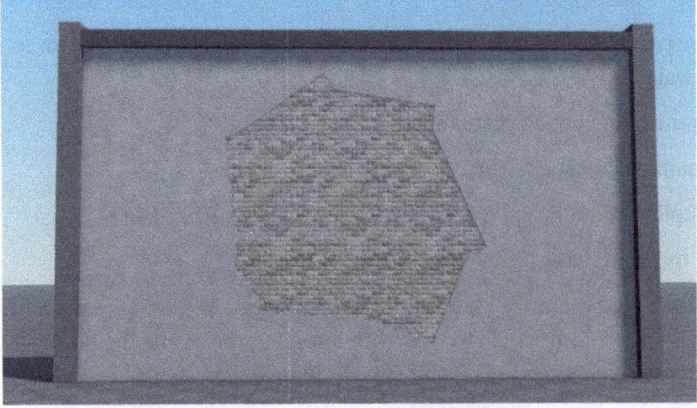

Figure 2.18: The hole in the wall

Let's now move on to the final recipe of this chapter, where we will learn how to sculpt low-poly rocks with the CSG tools.

From block to rock

In this recipe, we will be examining a way to turn a standard square block and sculpt it into a low-poly styled rock. Just as we cut a hole through the block by unioning a negated part to a normal part in the *Carving out Holes* recipe, we will use the same method to shave chunks off the block until we are satisfied with the look of our stone.

How to do it...

We will begin by creating a large generic base shape for our rock. We will then position several negated parts, rotated at various degrees and angles throughout the base rock part. We will then union the negated pieces with the original rock, giving us our low-poly look. To do this, follow these steps:

1. Insert a part, preferably a square one, into the Workspace. This will be the rock base shape.
2. Rescale the part to make it into your desired shape. For this example, I am creating a tall rock with a size of 27, 41, and 25 studs. Remember that the inserted part can easily be rescaled later, and that this process is usually quicker if you work with larger pieces when you carve the inserted part.
3. Duplicate the rock part and rotate it to a steep degree, ensuring that it intersects with the original rock. It should have a clean entry and exit, as shown in *Figure 2.19*:

Figure 2.19: The correctly intersected part

4. Now, negate the duplicated rock.

5. Select the negated part and the rock base, and union them both together. This will result in a nice slice being taken out of the rock wherever the parts intersected.
6. Place more negated parts along varying angles of the rock part.
7. Next, union the negated parts. Continue this step until you are satisfied with the look of your rock.
8. Enable **UsePartColor** in the property box of the union.
9. Now, you can modify the color of the rocks to 115, 115, and 115.
10. Change the material to **Slate**. This completes your low-poly rock models, created through the use of the CSG tools. It should leave you with something similar to *Figure 2.20*:

Figure 2.20: The finished low-poly rocks

That concludes the final recipe of this chapter on solid modeling.

By completing the recipes contained in this chapter, you can now feel confident that you know and understand how to use the different CSG tools, such as **negating**, **unioning**, and **intersecting**. Understanding how to effectively smooth-model on Roblox is a piece of powerful knowledge that will help you throughout your entire building career on this platform.

3
Sculpting Terrain

In this chapter, we will delve into the world of smooth terrain modeling in Roblox Studio, also known as **Voxel Terrain**. This allows you to create beautiful and realistic landscape environments for your games. With the help of various sculpting tools found in the **Terrain Editor** area, you can easily manipulate the terrain and apply different materials to it.

We will be using three different methods to create our terrain. First, we'll use the **Terrain Generator** tool; then, we'll use **Heightmap**; and finally, we'll hand-sculpt our landscape with the help of the **Part to Terrain** plugin. By the end of this chapter, you will have the knowledge and expertise to quickly create stunning landscapes that you can sculpt and adapt to suit your game's needs.

To that end, we will cover these recipes in this chapter:

- Generating large biomes
- Creating large terrain landscapes from scratch
- Stamping terrain with heightmap images
- Modifying terrain properties
- Hand-sculpting hills
- Creating an island in the ocean
- Creating a desert landscape
- Creating a mountain with a waterfall
- Sculpting an erupted volcano

Technical requirements

For this chapter, you will need the latest version of Roblox Studio downloaded (at the time of writing, this is version 594).

In this chapter, we will be working with **Terrain Editor** and its tools to create large landscapes of voxel terrain. Open it by navigating to the **Home** tab and selecting **Editor**. You will also need to download the **Heightmap** image, which can be found in the `Chapter 3` folder at `https://packt.link/gbz/9781805121596`, as well as the **Part to Terrain** plugin, which can be downloaded from `roblox.com/library/261634767`.

Generating large biomes

One aspect of a successful virtual experience is the cohesive, immersive world it brings to the player. For example, the thoughtfully designed worlds within games such as *Dungeon Quest* and *Vesteria* made for an unforgettable adventure throughout a multitude of environmental biomes, each with a theme and bosses.

A biome is a large area characterized by its vegetation, soil, and climate. There are five major types of biomes in Roblox Studio: aquatic, grassland, forest, desert, and tundra. Using **Terrain Generator** can be beneficial for several reasons. Firstly, it can save a considerable amount of time compared to hand-sculpting large areas of terrain. It can also provide a level of randomness and variation that is difficult to achieve when hand-sculpting. Let's look at how we can best use this tool.

Getting ready

Open **Roblox Studio**, create a new experience, and then delete the baseplate. Next, open **Editor** from the **Home** tab found within the top bar of Roblox Studio.

How to do it…

In this example, we will be using the **Terrain Generator** tool, which can be found in **Terrain Editor**. To do this, we will open the **Editor** menu and select the parameters that we want our terrain to generate. Let's see how we can quickly create a plot of landscape:

1. Open **Terrain Editor** and select the **Generate** icon under the **Create** tab.

2. In the **Map Settings** box, type in the position in which you want your terrain to spawn. In most cases, you can leave the numbers at 0, 0, 0, which will then generate the terrain in the center of the world space.

3. Next, you can modify the **Size** input box to the dimensions that you want your terrain to be generated at. If you're unsure what exact size you need, insert a square part and stretch it to the approximate size you wish your landscape to be. Next, check the size of the parts in the property box, and then translate the *X*, *Y*, and *Z* dimensions into the corresponding input boxes within **Terrain Editor**.

4. Under the **Material** setting drop-down section, choose what sort of biomes you want to generate in your map. Simply select the different attribute boxes. The more attribute boxes you have selected, the wider the variety of biomes that will be generated.

5. You can select the **Caves** toggle at the bottom of the **Material Settings** section if you would like caves to be randomly generated within your map terrain.
6. Click **Generate** and allow Roblox Studio to create your landscape:

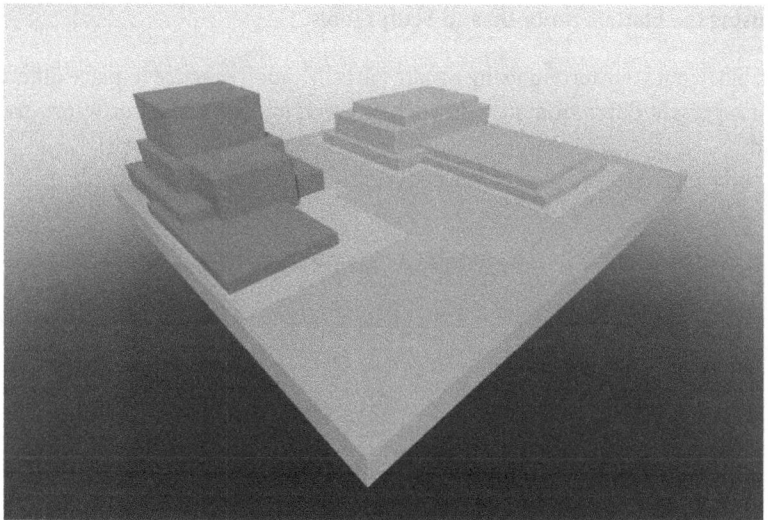

Figure 3.1: Generated landscape

There's more...

If you have **Seed Number** information, you can insert it in the bottom box in the **Other Settings** dropdown of the Terrain Generator window. A seed allows you to create reproducible streams of random numbers, meaning you're able to save your seed number and paste it in later; this will generate a replication of the terrain. For example, if you wanted to get the same terrain as what I generated, you would use seed `618033988`.

To play your world, exit the editor and then insert a spawn location by selecting **Spawn** inside the **Model** tab. Next, select the **Play** button (*F5*) inside the **Test** tab.

Creating large terrain landscapes from scratch

There are instances where utilizing a biome generator to create a large piece of terrain may not be the best option, especially when you have a very specific style, shape, or layout in mind for your landscape. In these situations, it is beneficial to know how to manually create large terrains using the **Part to Terrain** plugin. This plugin allows you to convert individual parts into terrain, allowing for greater control over the size, shape, and placement of each terrain chunk. Let's see how we can use this plugin and how we can then delve into the art of sculpting terrain to achieve the desired look. By manually sculpting the terrain, you will have complete control over the final product.

How to do it...

We will begin by blocking out the shape of our landscape using square parts. Next, we will use the **Part to Terrain** plugin to convert the parts into smooth terrain. We will then go through and smooth out the terrain using the **Flatten**, **Smooth**, and **Sculpt** tools:

1. To begin, block out your terrain using square parts. It's good practice to place different colored parts that represent different materials, such as green for grass, blue for water, gray for rock, and so on:

    Figure 3.2: Colored parts placed in the shape of our landscape

2. Next, open the **Part to Terrain** plugin and select what material you would like to convert your parts to from the pop-up menu. Begin clicking on each of the parts that you placed to convert them into smooth terrain:

    Figure 3.3: The terrain that's created after converting the parts into terrain

3. Now that you have successfully created the shape and size for your landscape, you may notice that there are areas in it that are not level, are unnaturally straight, or are uneven. For this, use the **Smooth** tool inside the **Edit** tab in **Terrain Editor**. Select the tool and click and drag your mouse over the terrain you want to smooth out.

4. Sometimes, the smoothing tool may not apply to your use case. In that case, you can use the **Flatten** tool in **Terrain Editor** to create a flatter transition in the blend lines first, then use the **Smooth** tool afterward to clean it up:

Figure 3.4: Example of smooth compared to not smooth

5. Now, using the **Sculpt** tool, go through the remainder of your landscape and sculpt the height differences to create more variety in the landscape. You can switch between the **Add** and **Subtract** brush modes.
6. If you want to add a large chunk of terrain, use the **Draw** tool to brush on large strokes of terrain.
7. After using the **Draw** tool, you can then sculpt the newly added terrain to your desired shape and slope using the **Sculpt** tool.

   To blend different terrain material types, use the **Sculpt** tool and gently brush over the different regions of terrain with a different material than the one underneath using a **Brush Strength** setting of 0.1. Doing this will gradually layer up several types of terrain on top of one another, resulting in a more unique and complex landscape.

8. With the **Draw** tool set to **Base Size 1** and the **Rock** material selected, click on the grass to apply extruded rocks that make them stand out taller than the grass, giving it a more realistic and less painted-on look:

Figure 3.5: Landscape with rocks scattered

There's more...

You can select regions of terrain to copy, paste, and/or duplicate entire land masses to expand on your terrain. To do so, first, navigate to the **Select** tool to select your region of terrain and position it by moving the modifier arrows to move and rotate the terrain. Next, use the **Transform** tool to modify the region as needed.

Stamping terrain with heightmap images

A **heightmap** is an image that illustrates the height and depth of a map's 3D terrain from a bird's-eye-view. The lighter areas of a heightmap correspond to higher elevations such as hills and mountains, while the darker areas correspond to lower elevations such as valleys and craters.

In this recipe, we will be utilizing heightmaps and colormaps to quickly and automatically stamp (generate) a variety of terrain types, including mountains, valleys, and lakes. We will then use a colormap to apply the materials across our stamped terrain.

Getting ready

For this, you will need a heightmap and a colormap. You can use any `png` image file, so long as it's grayscale, 18-bit, and has a top-down perspective. Alternatively, you may use the one provided in `chapter 3 Model Pack`.

How to do it...

To begin this recipe, we will open **Terrain Editor**, go to the **Import** tab, and then upload our heightmap to stamp out our landscape. Once the heightmap has been generated, we will then upload the colormap image into the Terrain Generator to give our terrain color and materials. Follow these steps:

1. First, open the **Import** tool under the **Create** tab of **Terrain Editor** and click on the **Import File** box to open your file browser.
2. Select and import the image of the heightmap from your file browser.
3. Select the material that you would like to generate as the default. In this example, we are using the **Rock** material.
4. Click the **Generate** button:

Figure 3.6: Mountain range created using a heightmap

5. Select the **Colormap** upload box, then choose your **Colormap** image to import it.
6. Click the **Generate** button. Your map will now have color, like so:

Figure 3.7: Finished colormap

Modifying terrain properties

In this recipe, we will dive deeper into the customization options available for Roblox terrain by modifying the properties of one of our previously created landscapes. We will explore the various ways to modify water properties, such as adjusting **Color**, **Transparency**, and **Reflection**. Additionally, we will learn how to modify texture, enabling us to create a landscape that matches our game's theme and setting. Furthermore, we will explore the **Decoration** feature, which will help take our game's visual quality to the next level.

How to do it...

For this task, we will be working with the terrain that we created in any of the previous recipes. We will begin by selecting the **Terrain** object located within the **Workspace** area of the **Explorer** window. We will be working within the **Properties** window to modify various settings on our terrain. We will start by applying grass decoration, and then modify the water's **Transparency**, **Reflection**, and **Wave Size**. To do this, follow these steps:

1. First, select the **Terrain** object found inside of the **Workspace** area, then navigate to the **Properties** window.

2. You can change the wind direction if your terrain's **Decoration** property is enabled. In the **View** tab, select **Wind Direction**. This will open a popup, which will allow you to adjust the slider to add wind. You can also select and rotate the blue arrow and green circle to change the direction and angle of the wind.

3. To modify the grass's height, select the **Terrain** object located in the **Workspace** area. In the **property** box, change **GrassLength** to 0.4:

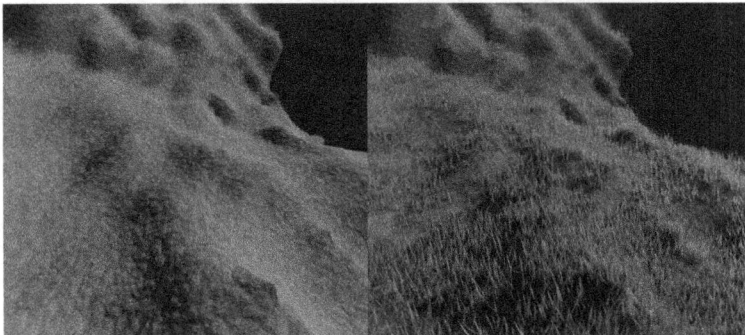

Figure 3.8: The difference between enabling decoration

4. Next, we will change our water properties in the **Appearance** tab located inside the **Properties** box. Navigate to the **Water Color** property and open the drop-down tab by clicking the arrow on the left of **Material**.

5. You can either input an RGB key code into the color input box or click the **Color** box to open the color pop-up menu.

6. Change **WaterReflectance** to a number between 0 and 1. This will adjust how much light will be reflected off the surface of the water. The higher the value, the shinier the water.

7. Modify **WaterTransparency** to a number between 0 and 1. This will change how deep into the water you can visibly see. The higher the transparency, the clearer the water, as depicted in *Figure 3.9*. When its transparency is set to 1, the water is very clear.

   Note that if you're not seeing any visible changes to your water as you change the value, read the *Important note* box found at the end of this recipe:

Figure 3.9: Water reflection and transparency differences

There are a few other features you can play around with to provide further realism for your bodies of water:

- **WaterWaveSize** changes the size of the waves. The larger the number, the larger the waves.
- **WaterWaveSpeed** changes the speed at which the waves move. The larger the number, the faster the water will ripple.

How it works...

Each material has its own set of physical attributes and has a corresponding RGB color assigned to it. Note that if Roblox Studio does not have the exact color key available from your color map, the closest matching material will be used automatically.

> **Important note**
> Since certain water properties are only visible while playtesting, you will need to set **Editor Quality Level** to the highest possible setting. This setting can be found by navigating to Roblox Studio's settings (*Alt + S*) and searching for `editor quality level` in the search box.

Hand-sculpting hills

For smaller scenes, where generating terrain is not applicable, you need to hand-sculpt the terrain to get the desired shape and size. In this recipe, we will be delving into the art of hand-sculpting. Specifically, we will be creating rolling hills with a cobblestone path. We will be using the various sculpting tools available in Roblox Studio's **Terrain Editor** to shape and manipulate the terrain to create realistic, visually pleasing hills. Additionally, we will discuss the importance of creating well-designed paths within the map to ensure players can navigate the landscape without getting lost.

How to do it…

We will be using various tools to create a visually appealing pathway through a grassy hill. We will fill in a flat region of grass, and then use the **Sculpt** tool to create hills of varying sizes. Next, we will use the **Paint** tool to create a path that we will detail with cobblestone terrain material. After, we will decorate the path with trees and rocks and finish off by adjusting **Global Lighting** and applying **DepthOfField** and **SunRays** objects into the **Lighting** object. To do so, follow these steps:

1. To begin, create a flat plain of grass by selecting an area with **Selection Tool** from the **Edit** tab. Click the **Fill** button to fill with grass material.

2. Using the **Sculpt** tool with **Brush Size** set to 25 and the **Grass** material selected, brush over the grass plane to create some hills of varying size by clicking on the grass plane to raise its elevation.

3. Now, with the **Paint** tool and the **Mud** material selected with **Brush Size** set to 6, paint on a path leading through your grassy hills.

4. With the **Paint** tool and the **Ground** material selected with **Brush Size** set to 4, paint in between the mud path you just created. This will give it a more unique materially layered appearance.

5. Using the **Paint** tool with **Brush Size** set to 2, lightly paint on blotches of **Cobblestone** material inside the bounds of the **Mud** material and **Ground** material that you previously painted on. The more cobblestone, the more visible the path will be:

Figure 3.10: Completed path after applying cobblestone

6. Using either **Toolbox** or `chapter 3 Model Pack`, insert the vegetation model pack. We will be placing vegetation and trees in a way that forms a wall along both sides of the path, which helps lead players toward the direction they need to go. Do not place trees or vegetation on the path – try to keep it spaced back a few studs from each edge of the dirt path. Trees should vary in size and stagger as perfectly aligned trees look unnatural.

7. After the trees have been placed, place the bush mesh plants in between the spacing of the trees, filling in the voids and adding density to the forest. The further away from the path, the larger the tree/vegetation can be:

Hand-sculpting hills 51

Figure 3.11: Bushes placed between the pine trees to obscure visibility, creating a "wall" along the path

8. Using the **Sculpt** tool with **Brush Size** set to 1, place rocks beside the path roughly three to six studs from the edge of the path. The **Sculpt** tool adds terrain in extruded clumps, which looks more like rock compared to the flat look you get by applying the **Rock** material with the **Paint** tool.
9. Enable the check box for the **DepthOfField** object located inside the **Lighting** object.
10. In the **Properties** box of **DepthOfField**, edit **NearIntensity** and **FarIntensity** until it creates a slight but not overly aggressive blur.
11. Right-click the **Lighting** object and insert **SunRayEffect**.
12. Select **SunRayEffect** inside the **Lighting** object and adjust the **Intensity** value in the **Properties** box of **SunRayEffect** to create a higher light beam shine.
13. You can modify the position of the global shadows by adjusting the number in the **GeographicLatitude** property found in the **Properties** box of the **Lighting** object to adjust where the sun is positioned in the sky. This affects the positioning and length of object shadows.

As shown in *Figure 3.12*, our lighting and shadow properties greatly improve the map's realism:

Figure 3.12: Finished screenshot of hand-sculpted hills with a path

Creating an island in the ocean

In this recipe, we will use the **Part to Terrain** plugin to create a custom island in the water. We will begin by grayboxing the basic shape of the island with parts and then use the **Terrain Editor** tools to sculpt and refine the terrain. We will then create an ocean surrounding the island and adjust its size and sea level to achieve the desired level. Additionally, we will cover how to add micro details to the sand and rock formations by using the provided **Sculpt** tool. By the end of this recipe, you'll have a beautiful, handcrafted island.

How to do it…

We will begin this recipe by creating a sandy baseplate that we will then draw on the shape of our island using the **Add** tool. Next, we will flatten out the perimeter of the island using the **Flatten** tool, and then add water using **Sea Level Generator**. To finish the island, we will paint grass on top, precisely scatter rocks around the perimeter, and then paint on splashed sand. To start, follow these steps:

1. Spawn in a square part and change its size to 2048, 8, 2048 studs, or use the default baseplate located in the **Workspace** area. Change the material type to **sand** and the color to 165, 143, 86. Since we won't be touching this part again, we can lock it by equipping the **Lock** tool (*Ctrl + L*) and then click on the part to lock/unlock it.

2. Next, use the **Selection** tool to draw out a square the rough size of your island. Next, select the **Fill** tool and then select the **sand** material. Click **Apply.**

3. In the **Edit** tab of **Terrain Editor**, select the **Sculpt** tool with **Brush Size** set to 6 with **Subtract** mode enabled. Now, looking top-down at the baseplate, brush on the outline of your island. As shown in *Figure 3.13*, this will help you gradually sculpt the square terrain into your desired shape.

4. Using the **Flatten** tool in **Terrain Editor** with **Base Size** set to 18, brush along the edges of the sand to flatten it. This will give us a smooth taper from our beach into the water:

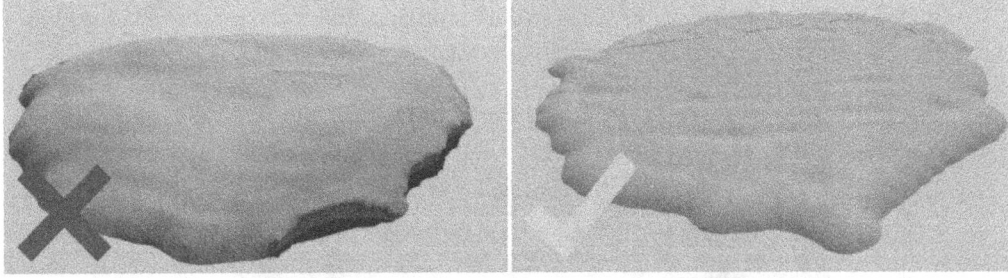

Figure 3.13: Incorrect and correctly flattened sand

5. Using the **Sculpt** tool with the **Grass** material and **Strength** set to 0.5, create an elevated grassy patch in the center of the island. Raise the terrain toward the back of the island.

6. Using the **Sculpt** tool with the **Ground** material selected, with **Base Size** set to 0.3 and **Strength** set to 0.1, brush over the top of the outskirts of the grass, applying a layer of terrain detail.

7. Select the **Add** option inside the **Sculpt** tool, change **Brush size** to 1, and select the **Rock** material. Click and carefully scatter rocks in and around the hill slope and on the more elevated back half of the island. Continue to scatter rocks around the hill to create a rocky cliff on the back half of your island.

8. In the **Edit** tab of **Terrain Editor**, select **Sea Level**, then change the bounding box to the position and size you wish to have for your ocean.

9. Click **Create** to generate the water:

Figure 3.14: Ocean being generated with the Sea Level tool in Terrain Editor

10. Select the **Paint** tool with **Brush Size** set to 1 with the **Limestone** material selected. Dab on small blotches of it along where the water meets the sand. You can also scatter some on the rocks and in the grass to make it look like sand has been washed up from the tide.

11. Select the **Terrain** object in the **Workspace** area and open the **MaterialColors** dropdown in the **property** box. Darken the color of the **Limestone** material to a darker shade, such as 184, 147, 116. It should now look like wet sand.

12. In the same **MaterialColors** drop-down menu, modify the color of the sand to be more orange-toned. I used 207, 185, 160 in this example.

13. Now, while still in the **Terrain property** box, modify the remaining terrain properties for both your water and terrain until you are satisfied. You now have a completed island that smoothly transitions into the sea. We can see the result of our island in *Figure 3.15*:

Figure 3.15: Finished island

There's more...

To take your island to the next level, you can apply an image decal to the seabed to make it look more realistic. In *Figure 3.16*, you can see how applying a decal of a coral reef to the underwater baseplate adds both depth and detail to the ocean:

Figure 3.16: Seabed decal

Creating a desert landscape

In this recipe, we will explore the process of creating a desert landscape in Roblox. We will start by creating a flat plain of terrain followed by the process of shaping it with the add and subtract options of the **Sculpt** tool. Then, we will focus on the sculpting tools we can use to create dunes and rock formations that accurately represent a desert environment. We will finish off the scene by adjusting the lighting settings and atmosphere to capture the essence of a barren, dry desert.

How to do it...

For this recipe, we will start by creating a stretch of flat sand with the **Selection** and **Fill** tools. We will then use the **Add** and **Sculpt** tools to create sand dunes and pillars. Next, we will block out a large dune mountain and convert it into smooth terrain with the **Part to Terrain** plugin. We will finish off by smoothing out the dunes with the **Smooth** and **Flatten** tools, then decorate the scene with cactuses. To begin, follow these steps:

1. Using the **Selection** tool of **Terrain Editor**, create a large flat plain then fill it with the **Sand** material.
2. Choose the **Sand** material at the bottom of **Terrain Editor** and click **Fill** at the bottom of the editor.
3. Using the **Sculpt** tool with the **Add** brush mode option selection, run the brush over the entirety of the sandy plane, holding it still in some areas to create dunes and unevenness on the sand plane.
4. Select the **Add** tool with **Base Size** set to 3 and choose the **Sandstone** material. With the camera facing top-down, click your mouse a few times in the same place to create pillars of sandstone. You can create pillars and arch shapes, making them look like wind-carved rock dunes, as displayed in *Figure 3.17*:

Figure 3.17: Sandstone pillars created with the Add tool

5. Insert a square part into the sand terrain and create a block-out of a mountain dune with a large overhanging arch, as seen in *Figure 3.18*.

6. Using the **Part to Terrain** plugin, convert the parts into **Sandstone** material:

Figure 3.18: The dune before and after converting the parts into terrain

7. Using the **Flatten** and **Smooth** tools, feather out and soften the sand around the base of the mountain dune, the same as we did in *Step 4* of the *Creating large terrain landscapes from scratch* recipe of this chapter.

8. At the top of the mountain dune, use the **Add** tool to create pillars of rock, as we did in *Step 4* of this recipe.

9. Next, select the **Lighting** object in the **Explorer** window. In the **Properties** box, change **Ambient Color** to `130, 128, 68`, and set **Brightness** to `6`.

10. Right-click the **Lighting** object and insert an **Atmosphere** object if there is not one inside it already.

11. In the **Properties** box of **Atmosphere**, change the atmosphere's **Density** to `0.444` and **Offset** to `0.72`.

> **Note**
> A higher density number equals thicker fog and less clarity.

12. Insert the cactuses that we built in the *Building cactuses* recipe of *Chapter 1*, or use the ones provided in `chapter 3 Model Pack`. Stagger them as you place them and ensure they're randomly rotated and vary in size so that they feel more natural and not just identical copy and pastes of one another.

The result is a large natural-looking desert biome scene containing natural-looking pillars of sandstone carved out in the wind, decorated with cactuses and other elements that make up this scene, as shown in *Figure 3.19*:

Figure 3.19: Finished desert scene

Creating a mountain with a waterfall

In this recipe, we will be creating a tall rocky mountain scene. We will begin by using the Terrain Generator to create a basic mountain valley, and then we will personalize it by hand-editing the terrain to give it a unique touch. The mountains will be tall and full of caves, pools of water, and other areas to explore. We will also learn how to create density with trees, and you will discover how to create a realistic-looking waterfall that flows down the mountainside by using the Waterfall plugin.

Getting ready

In this recipe, we will use a heightmap to stamp out a large mountain landscape. You will need to download your own heightmap or use the square heightmap image to generate the mountains, which can be found inside the `chapter 3 Model Pack` folder. You will also need the **Waterfall Generator** plugin installed from the Roblox plugin toolbox.

How to do it...

In this recipe, we will use a heightmap image to create the base landscape of the terrain. We will then go through and clean up the stamped terrain using various tools from **Terrain Editor**. Next, we will create an intricate cave system with pools of water, which are illuminated with point lights. To finish, we will use the **Waterfall Generator** plugin to create a waterfall from one of the caves down into a lake of water. To start, follow these steps:

1. Using either **Heightmap** or **Terrain Generator**, generate or stamp a region of mountainous terrain into the world space.

2. Now that we have created the mountains, some of them may need to be hand-sculpted to get the desired look. In this case, the mountains are too thin, so I will use the **Add** tool to thicken the mountains:

Figure 3.20: Using the Add tool to thicken the mountains

3. Next, use the **Sculpt** and **Smooth** tools to spread out and smooth the terrain that we placed with the **Add** tool in *Step 2*.
4. Now, use the **Sculpt** tool with the brush mode set on **Add**, and alternate between the **Ground**, **Grass**, and **Rock** materials to pull the terrain upwards while applying the layers of varying terrain.
5. Using the **Subtract** tool, carve out holes into the mountains to create some caves. You can connect the tunnels to create an intricate underground tunnel system.
6. Go through and use the **Sculpt** tool to grow out different materials and to make the shape less spherical, and instead a bit more natural.
7. Create some holes in the ceiling to allow natural light into the caves using the **Subtract** tool:

Figure 3.21: Light shining through cracks in the cave ceiling

8. Using the **Paint** tool with the **Water** material selected, paint water on the floor of one of the cave's areas, creating puddles and small pockets of water:

Figure 3.22: Stream of water pooling inside the cave

9. Insert a square part, and then insert **Point Light** into said part.
10. Change the part's **Transparency** to 1 and uncheck the **CanCollide** box so that players won't collide with the square part.
11. Place the square part in or around the water to illuminate it. This will give it a fun and unique glow that will attract players, as well as providing a source of light so that they can see inside the cave.
12. Next, we will create a waterfall streaming out from a cave into a pool of water. To do this, select the **Waterfall Generator** plugin and choose the options within its pop-up box to fit your style preference.
13. Once you've chosen your settings, click the box at the bottom of the popup – that is, **Click to generate the start of your waterfall**.
14. Click at the top of the waterfall where the waterfall begins, and then click at the bottom of the waterfall where you want it to end. You can adjust the position and rotation of the top and bottom of the waterfall by moving the **Plunge** and **Source** parts found in the **Waterfall** group located inside the **Workspace** area:

Figure 3.23: Waterfall coming out of the end of a cave

15. At the bottom of the waterfall, use the **Sculpt** tool with the brush mode set to **Subtract** to erode a hole in the lake.
16. In the bottom of the eroded hole, use the **Paint** tool with the **Sand** material selected and paint in a sand bed.
17. Using the **Selection** tool, click inside the hole and scale the selection box to fill the volume of the hole where you want the water to go.
18. Using the **Fill** tool, fill it with the **Water** material:

Figure 3.24: Finished lake with waterfall

19. Using the pine trees provided inside the `chapter 3 Model Pack` folder, place trees within the mountainy scape following the same principles for placing trees as in the *Modifying terrain properties* recipe of this chapter.

20. Right-click the **Lighting** object in **Explorer** and insert the **SunRays** object.

21. Inside the property box of **Lighting**, change **Ambient Top Color** to `60, 83, 36` and **Ambient Bottom Color** to `103, 130, 89`.

22. Inside the **Lighting** object, change **Atmosphere Density** to `350` or until you feel it fits the mood of your map.

The result should look something like what's shown in *Figure 3.25*:

Figure 3.25: Completed waterfall scene

Sculpting an erupted volcano

In this recipe, we will be building a night scene of a volcano overflowing with lava. We will start by using a biome generator to create the initial lava mountain, and then use our knowledge of terrain editing to add a walkable path for players to explore. We will also use Roblox's basic lighting tools to illuminate the lava and adjust the lighting settings to create a stunning night scene. By the end of this recipe, you will have a mesmeric volcano landscape.

How to do it...

We will start by creating a large flat volcano biome using the **Terrain Generator** tool. We will then build out the shape of the volcano using square parts, and then convert the parts into smooth terrain using the **Part to Terrain** plugin. Next, we will smooth out the terrain and hollow out the center of the volcano so that we can create a pool of lava inside. We will finish the scene by using the **Paint** and **Sculpt** tools to create a river of lava flowing from the sides of the volcano. To begin, follow these steps:

1. You can use the same mountain biome that we created in the *Creating a mountain with a waterfall* recipe or use the **Selection** and **Fill** tools to create a 1000, 300, 1000 size landscape. The seed we've used here is 618033988.

2. Select only the **Lavascape** option in the **Biome** checkbox fields.

3. Set **Biome Size** to 100.

4. Click **Generate**. This will generate the initial surface of the biome, which we will create the volcano on top of:

Figure 3.26: A generated volcano biome

5. Place some square parts around in the shape of a volcano. Keep a hole in the middle of the bricks for the lava to sit in. Rotate some of the parts at the bottom to create a slope so that it's a cleaner mountain transition to the ground, making it easier to climb:

Figure 3.27: Stepped parts shaped like a volcano

6. Using the **Part to Terrain** plugin, convert the parts into the **Rock** material.
7. Using the **Sculpt** tool with the **Rock** material selected, grow out the blocky layers of the volcano to smooth it out:

Figure 3.28: A comparison of smooth and non-smooth mountains

8. Changing between the **Basalt**, **Slate**, and **Asphalt** materials within the **Sculpt** tool, gently brush over the top of the rocky material to grow the new material from it, layering on detail:

Figure 3.29: Differing layers of material applied to the mountain using the Grow Terrain Editor tool

9. Widen the top hole of the volcano by using the **Subtract** and **Sculpt** tools, with the brush mode set to **Subtract**:

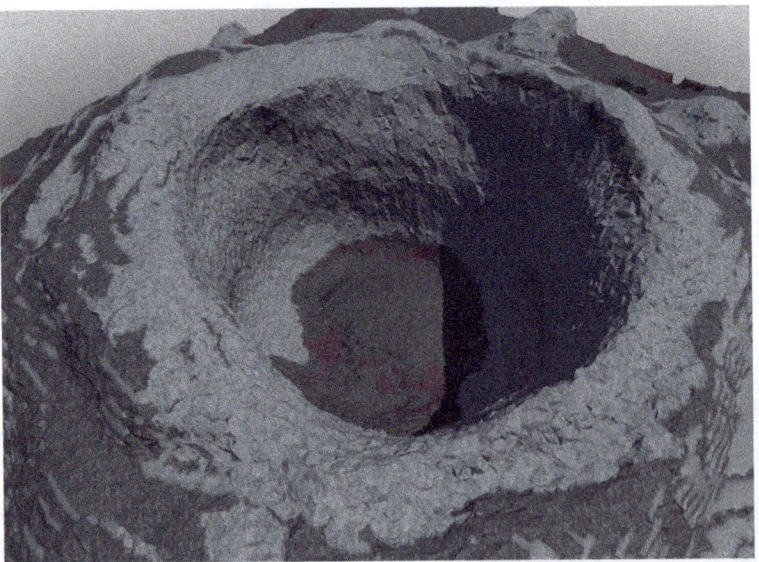

Figure 3.30: Carved hole created with the Erode tool

10. Inside the volcano, use the **Select** tool to drag out a region filling the pit where the lava will go.
11. Select the **Lava** material and click **Fill**.

12. Insert a square or cylinder part on top of the lava in the volcano and rescale it to fit the inside of the volcano.
13. Change the part's material to **Neon**.
14. Change the part's **Color** to orange (165, 97, 76).
15. Change the part's **Transparency** to 0.72.
16. Right-click the neon part and insert **Point Light**.
17. Change the point light's **Range** to 60 to illuminate the lava.
18. Change the point light's **Color** to orange (165, 97, 7).
19. Erode one of the sides of the volcano using the **Sculpt** tool with the brush mode set to **Subtract**.

Figure 3.31: An eroded path created for lava to flow down

20. Using the **Paint** tool, paint with the **Lava** material along the hole we made, down the side of the volcano to create a river of lava.
21. Select the **Sculpt** tool with the brush mode set to **Add** and the **Basalt** material chosen. Brush along the edges of your lava rivers so that it doesn't appear to be flatly painted on. This also helps create more natural-looking rivers of lava flowing.

After sculpting the rivers of lava, you will have a completed volcano scene:

Sculpting Terrain

Figure 3.32: Finished volcano scene

There's more...

If you want to give your lava some depth, use parts with .6 transparency and stack them on top of each other. This creates a stylized sense of depth in the pool of lava:

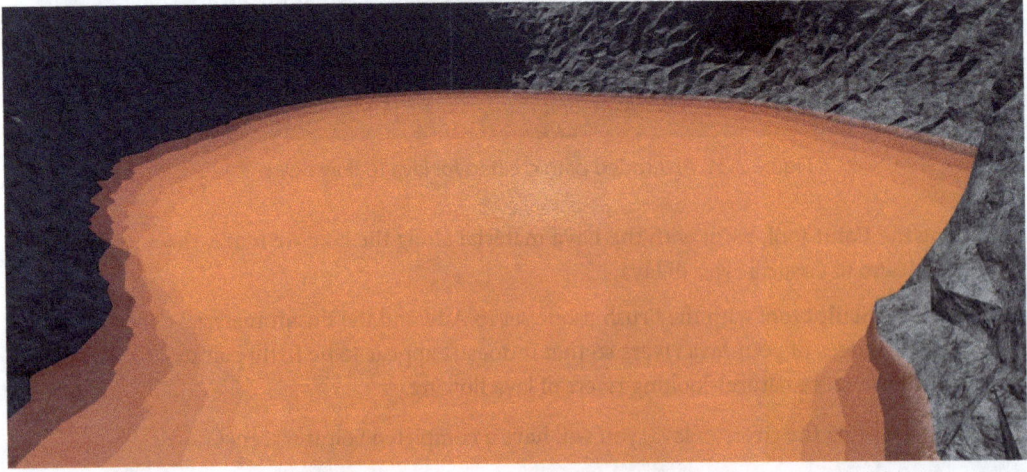

Figure 3.33: Layers of semi-transparent neon parts stacked on top of each other to create visual depth

4
Learning to Use VFX

Visual effects (**VFX**) are what can take a product from being good to spectacular. In this chapter, we will be learning the art of translating your imagination into VFX using the in-house options that Roblox provides, such as beams, particles, and trails. Each of these emits 2D images that we will customize the behavior of to get our desired look. We'll also be examining how to utilize the `FlipbookLayout` option within the `ParticleEmitter` property options. We will examine the best use cases for each effect as well as how to customize the various property options to give it a look that best suits our game's needs.

In this chapter, we will be examining the following recipes:

- Creating simple effects with fire, smoke, and sparkles
- Creating hi-res fire with particles
- Making volumetric smoke with particles
- Beaming a laser
- Flipbook particle explosion
- Trailing behind players
- Building a whirlwind
- Snowflakes falling from above

Technical requirements

You will need to open an empty baseplate in the latest version of Roblox Studio downloaded (at the time of writing, version 572). You will also need to toggle on the **Constraint Details** setting, found inside the **Model** tab.

In this chapter, we will be working with images and textures located here: https://packt.link/gbz/9781805121596.

Creating simple effects with fire, smoke, and sparkles

Roblox has several premade particle-emitting classes that allow us to instantly attach it to parts and attachments to give us a customizable effect. These premade particles have limited customizability but do serve a useful purpose. In this recipe, we will be examining how to apply and customize the three premade **ParticleEmitter** objects – **Sparkle**, **Fire**, and **Smoke**. We will be using these three effects to construct a simple fire pit. *Figure 4.1* shows the three default effects side by side:

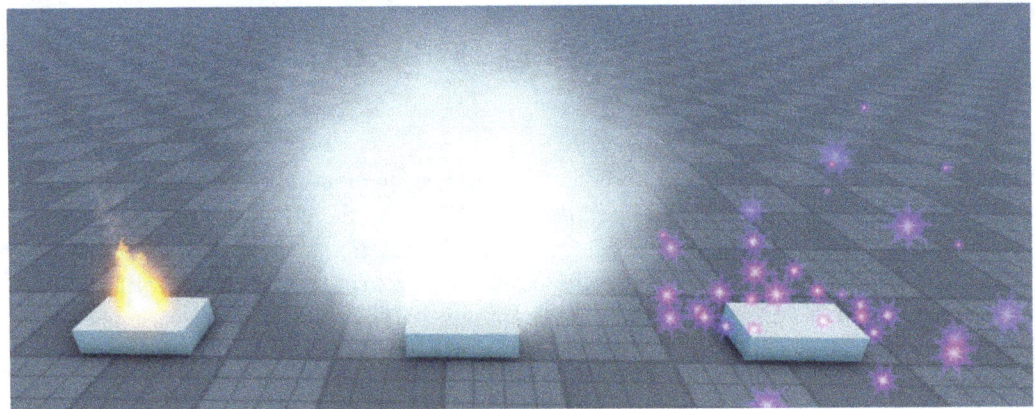

Figure 4.1: Fire, smoke, and sparkle effects

How to do it...

We will start by inserting a square part and then scaling it into the shape of a log. After duplicating the log, we will rotate and stack the logs on top of one another. We will then add color and the **Wood** material to it, then insert **Fire**, **Smoke**, and **Sparkle** effects from the **Effects** drop-down menu. We will then go through each of the effects one by one and see how to best customize them. To begin, follow these steps:

1. Insert a square part and then rescale it into the rectangular shape of a log, about `5.5`, `1`, `1` studs.
2. Now, change the log's color to `80`, `57`, `74`.
3. Change the log's material to **Wood**. If the woodgrain is running in the wrong direction, then you can use the **Material Flip** plugin to correct it.
4. Duplicate the part twice and stack the logs as shown in *Figure 4.2*:

Figure 4.2: Wood stack

5. Select the original part that's flat on the ground, then navigate to the **Effects** drop-down menu found inside the **Model** tab within the top bar of the studio.

   The particle will be emitted at the angle at which the part sits, which is why it's important to keep the part that you plan to add the particle to flat on the baseplate. Otherwise, insert the effect into an invisible part placed in the logs.

6. Select the **Fire** effect in the **Effects** drop-down menu to insert it into the part. You should now have a flame emitting from the first block.

7. Now that we have the fire emitter inserted, we will modify the fire's properties. To start, select the **Fire** object found inside the part.

8. In the property box, change **Heat** to 8. The higher the number, the taller the flame height will be.

9. Now, change the **Size** value to 9. This will change the overall flame size.

10. Finally, change the **TimeScale** property value to 0.65. The lower the number, the slower the flame animation will play. Congrats – you now have a burning pile of wood!

Figure 4.3: Burning wood pile

11. Now, select the part that has the **Fire** object and insert the **Smoke** effect from the **Effects** drop-down menu.
12. Change the **Opacity** value to `0.1`. The higher the number, the denser the smoke.
13. Change the **RiseVelocity** property value to `10`. The higher the number, the faster the smoke will rise.
14. Now, change the **Size** value to `0.25`.
15. Change the **TimeScale** property value to `0.45` to slow down the speed of the smoke.
16. Now, insert the **Sparkle** effect into the same part that has fire and smoke inside.
17. Change the sparkles' **TimeScape** property value to `0.15`.
18. Now, change the **SparkleColor** property value to the same color as the fire – in this case, `255, 110, 105`.
19. Select the part and insert a **Pointlight** object.
20. Change the **Range** value of the pointlight to `12`.
21. Set the pointlight's **Brightness** value to `3`.
22. Finally, change the pointlight's **Color** value to `255, 110, 105`. You now have a completed fireplace created with basic fire, smoke, and sparkle particle effects provided in the studio:

Figure 4.4: Finished fire

See how easy it was to quickly modify the built-in particle emitters that Studio has? Although it was fast to implement, the available options to customize these simple effects are minimal. Let's continue to the next recipe, which will dive deeper into the creation of particle effects from scratch using the **ParticleEmitter** object!

Creating hi-res fire with particles

ParticleEmitter is one of the more used types of effects because it allows for a wide range of effects. Particles are great for making anything, from splashing water, smoke, and dust specks to fire. In this recipe, we will be examining a method to create a more stylized fire with embers emitting from it using the Roblox **ParticleEmitter** object, versus using the basic effects from *Creating simple effects with fire, smoke, and sparkles* recipe.

How to do it...

After inserting a **ParticleEmitter** object into a transparent part, we will insert our **ImageID** texture. Next, we will modify the color and transparency using **Sequence Graph**. We will then modify various parameters within the property box to get our desired look. To begin, follow these steps:

1. Create a stack of logs. Right-click on one of the parts and insert a **ParticleEmitter** object.
2. Rename the particle emitter `Fire`.
3. Set the original part's **Transparency** value to `1`.
4. Select the **ParticleEmitter** object inside of the part inside **Workspace**.
5. In the **Texture** box, paste the **ImageID** texture of the fire that you would like to use. A couple of IDs that you can try are **Stylized Fire** (`2282042320`) and **Realistic Fire** (`248625108`).

    Figure 4.5 shows how both effects look while active:

    Figure 4.5: Stylized and realistic textures

6. With the size set, change the color of the flame by clicking the three-dotted icon on the right side of the color box. This will open the **Color Sequence** graph box.
7. Click the triangles at the bottom of the color graph, then select a color in the color square popup. In this example, I am using the `248, 64, 32` color.

Learning to Use VFX

8. You can add more triangles (keyframes) by clicking on the graph, and delete them by hitting the *Delete* key on your keyboard. You can also select and drag the triangles, which will in turn affect the gradient. In this example, I added more keyframes through the middle of the graph to create a gradient effect:

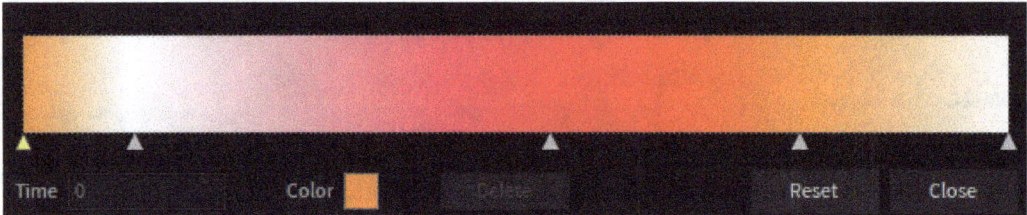

Figure 4.6: Transparency graph

9. Now, change the **Speed** number value to 7, allowing the flames to rise faster.
10. Next, change the **LifeTime** number value to 0.5, 1.5. This will cause particles to appear for between 0.5 seconds and 1.5 seconds before disappearing.
11. Now, select the three-dotted icon beside the **Transparency** property to open the transparency box.
12. Click and drag the square on the right side of the graph and drag it to the very top, giving it a **Transparency** value of 1. Now, the fire will fade out smoothly rather than randomly disappearing.
13. Modify the **Rate** value at which the particles are being emitted. In this example, the number value is 65.
14. Next, change the **Size** value of the particle by selecting the three-dotted icon beside the **Size** box. This will open the **Size** popup.
15. Next, select and then drag the black square on the right side of the graph down so that its value is 0. Now, the particles will gradually shrink as they rise. Now that you have a basic fire, let's add some embers.
16. Duplicate the **ParticleEmitter** object inside of the part and name the object Embers.
17. Change the **Size** value of the ember particles to 0.1.
18. Set the **Squash** value to 0.1; this will compress the shape of the particle slightly.
19. Change the **Lifetime** values to 0.75 and 2.
20. Now, open the **Transparency Graph** box and set the left square's value to 0.85 and the right square's value to 1.
21. Next, insert a **Pointlight** object into the log.
22. Set the pointlight's **Range** value to 15.

23. Finally, set the pointlight's **Brightness** value to 3. You now have successfully created your first two particle emitters from scratch!

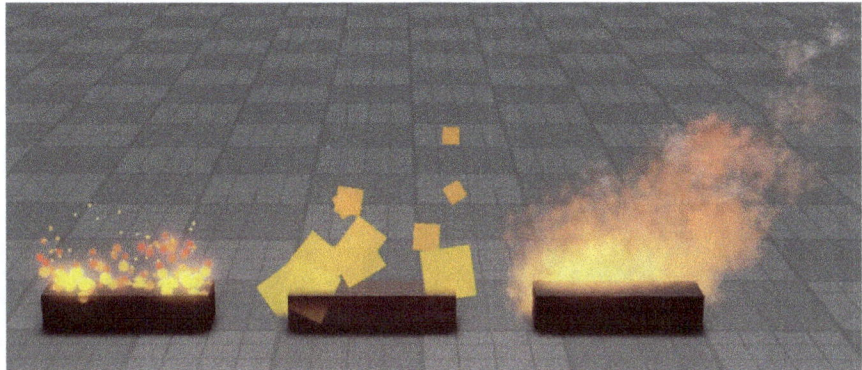

Figure 4.7: Finished stylized fire variants

After completing this recipe, you now know how to work with the basic properties of particle emitters such as squash, lifetime, and size. You also learned how to navigate the color sequence box as well as the transparency graph, which will come in handy throughout the remaining recipes. Next, we will examine how to create a volumetric cloud using particles. Let's see how.

Making volumetric smoke with particles

Another great use case for particle emitters is creating volumetric smoke. In this recipe, we will be going through the step-by-step procedure to create a large puff of slowly rolling smoke. This method is also applicable for creating VFX such as gas, mist, dust, and fog.

How to do it...

We will begin by inserting a **ParticleEmitter** object into a square part. Next, we will insert our **ImageID** texture and then set up the **LightEmission** and **LightInfluence** property options. We will then modify the size and transparency of the smoke, and then finish the recipe by applying a slight rotation. To start, follow these steps:

1. Insert a square part into **Workspace**, and then set its **Transparency** value to `1`.
2. Set the part's **CanCollide** property value to `False`.
3. Next, rescale the part to be `80, 30, 80` studs.
4. Right-click the part and insert a **ParticleEmitter** object.
5. Rename the **ParticleEmitter** object `Smoke`.
6. Insert the **ImageID** texture for the smoke. In this example, the ID is `rbxas-setid://10186762664`.

7. Change the **LightEmission** property value to `0.4`. The higher the value, the more light will be emitted from the particle, lighting it up brighter.
8. Change the **LightInfluence** property value to `1`. This will allow other environments' light to influence the appearance of the smoke:

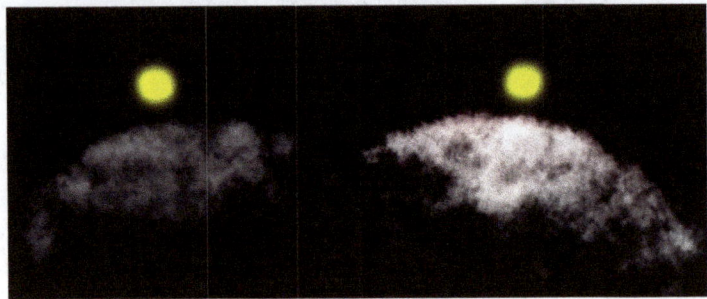

Figure 4.8: Light influence 0 versus 1 with a PointLight emitting over the top

9. Next, set the **Size** value of the particles to `35`.
10. Make sure that the **Orientation** option is set to `FacingCamera`.
11. Change the **LifeTime** property value to `9`.
12. Open the **Transparency Graph** box and move the right and left squares to the very top, giving them both a value of `1`.
13. About one-third of the way through the graph, click to insert another keyframe.
14. Set the new keyframe's value to `0.92`.
15. Now, change the **Rotation** value to `-180, 180`, which will cause the smoke to roll in on itself.
16. Change the **RotSpeed** property value to `15`. The higher the number, the quicker the smoke will rotate based on the increments that we used in *step 14*.
17. Finally, change the **SpreadAngle** property value to `90, 90` to allow the smoke to feather out. You now have a cloud of smoke bound within the set perimeters created from scratch using a single particle emitter:

Figure 4.9: Finished smoke particle effect

By finishing this recipe, you have deepened your knowledge of how to modify particles. You learned why and how to apply rotation and spread. You also learned the steps to create a dense cloud and how to keep it from looking flat and bland to reflective and delicate. Let's now look at how we can use the **Beam** object to create a laser in the following recipe.

Beaming a laser

A second resource that Roblox provides us with is the **Beam** object, which draws a texture between two attachments. Attachments define a point we can use to create a start and end point for the beam. We can then modify the appearance of the image being emitted, the curvature, and the width to create a tight beam effect. We will examine how to create attachments and then how to project a beam between the two set attachment points.

How to do it...

We will start this recipe by inserting two **Attachment** objects into a part and then moving them to the width of our beam. We will then insert a **Beam** object and then link it to the two attachments. We will continue by applying our **ImageID** texture and then changing the start and end width of the beam. To begin, follow these steps:

1. In the top menu bar, navigate to the **Constraints** section found under the **Model** tab.
2. Enable **Constraint Details** so that the constraints that we place are visible.
3. Next, insert a square part and scale it into a `1, 1, 1`-stud cube.
4. Right-click on the square part, then select **Insert Object…**.
5. Select the **Attachment** object.
6. Select the **Attachment** object inside of the part and then duplicate it.
7. Move one of the attachments about 30 studs over; this will be the length of the beam, as shown in *Figure 4.10*:

Figure 4.10: Beam stretching between attachments

8. Rename one of the attachments `Start`, and the other one `Finish`.
9. Next, right-click on the part and then select **Insert Object…**.
10. Select the **Beam** object to insert it.
11. In the beam's property box under the **Shape** tab, click **Attachment0**, then select the attachment in **Workspace** that we named **Start**.

12. As in *step 11*, click **Attachment1** inside of the beam's property box, then select the attachment we named **Finish**.
13. Enable **FaceCamera**.
14. Next, insert your **ImageID** texture into the **Texture** box. Try these different IDs out for different beam styles:

    - rbxassetid://15288609122
    - rbxassetid://15288610363
    - rbxassetid://15288581962
    - rbxassetid://15288583813

15. Change the **LightEmission** property value to 1. The higher the value, the more the beam will blend with the colors behind it. Next, set the **LightInfluence** property value to 0.3. The higher the value, the more the beam will be affected by the environment's lighting.
16. Change the **TextureSpeed** property value to 3. This will increase how fast the texture travels from one attachment to the next.
17. Change the number value of **Width0** to 2. This will change the width of this side's texture.
18. Now, change the number value of **Width1** to 4.
19. Open the **Transparency Graph** and select the black square on the left side of the graph. Change the first square's value to 0.
20. Finally, select the other black square on the right side of the graph and change its value to 0.3. This will create a gradient that gradually fades from a 0 to 0.3 transparency. That concludes this recipe. You now have a basic knowledge of how beams work!

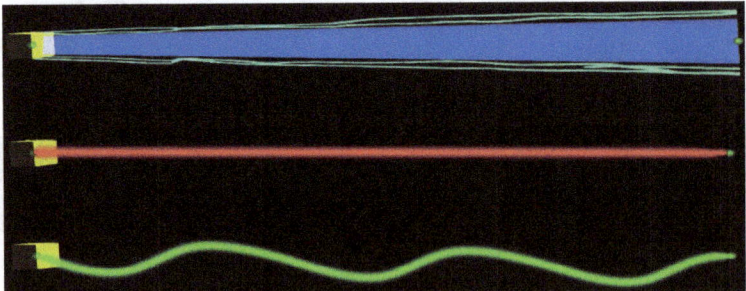

Figure 4.11: Finished laser beams

After completing these steps, you should now be confident in your skills in creating beams. You effectively set up the attachments and then hooked them up to the beam emitter. You then saw how changing the speed and width of the texture affects the look, as well as setting up a transparent gradient. Let's now look at a more advanced method for creating VFX in the next recipe.

Flipbook particle explosion

Flipbook textures, also known as **Animated Textures**, are a type of particle emitter. When enabled, they allow you to use sprite sheets to animate the texture of the particle over the duration of its lifetime. This is very useful for creating high-quality and consistently animated effects such as explosions, fire, power-ups, and more. Let's see how we can create and upload our own sprite sheet into a high-quality explosive effect. We will be using 1024x1024 textures laid out into flipbook frames. Currently, only 2x2, 4x4, and 8x8 layouts are compatible with Roblox.

How to do it...

After inserting a **ParticleEmitter** object into an invisible part, we will change the property of the emitter to **FlipbookLayout**. This will allow us to set our grid size and then import our flipbook frame sprite sheet. We will then modify the various values of the emitter's properties to create a stunning visual. To start, follow these steps:

1. First, begin by inserting a square part onto the baseplate.
2. Change the part's **Transparency** value to `1`.
3. Anchor the part so that it cannot move.
4. Select the part and insert a **ParticleEmitter** object into it.
5. Inside the property box of **ParticleEmitter** under the **Flipbook** tab, change the **FlipbookLayout** property value to `Grid8x8`, or whatever grid size your texture is. For example, if it's an 8x8 grid, then the texture will have 64 images on the sheet.
6. Insert a 1024x1024 flipbook frame into the **Texture** box of **ParticleEmitter**. You can use a 2x2, 4x4, or an 8x8 layout for the texture. For this example, you can use one of the following:

    - `rbxassetid://8081544635`
    - `rbxassetid://15295160682`
    - `rbxassetid://15295178805`
    - `rbxassetid://15295179618`
    - `rbxassetid://15295193846`
    - `rbxassetid://15295194323`

    You can see an example of a standard 8x8 flipbook effect for an explosion in *Figure 4.12*:

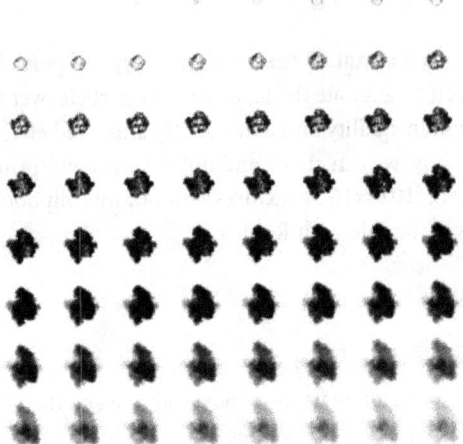

Figure 4.12: Example of a 64-frame flipbook layout

7. Change the **Size** value to 6, or the size you desire.
8. Next, change the **Lifetime** value to 8, 12. Having two number (*8* and *12*) values will randomize the times that the particle exists before it fades. This will help it look more organic and less repetitive.
9. Change the **Rate** value to 1.
10. Set the **Rotation** value to -60, 120. This will cause the particle to rotate versus staying static.
11. Change the **RotSpeed** property value to 10. The higher the number value, the faster the particle will rotate.
12. Change the **Speed** value to 1. This value will change how fast the particle will travel in studs per second; so, for example, in this case, the particle would be traveling at 1 stud per second.
13. Change the **SpreadAngle** property value to 15, 15. The higher the numbers, the further the range that the particle will spread.
14. Change the **Acceleration** value to 0, 0.1, 0. This will move the particles upward along the *y* axis.
15. Now, open the **Transparency Graph** box.
16. Set both the left and right square keyframe's value to 0.7.
17. Insert a keyframe with a value of 0.05 just slightly past the first keyframe by clicking on the graph.
18. Insert another keyframe with a value of 0.05 just before the keyframe on the far right end. You should now have four keyframes in total going from 0.7 -> 0.05 -> 0.05 -> 0.7 in values.
19. Finally, change the **LightEmission** property value to 0.15. This completes the last step of this recipe; you should now be left with the skills to create and edit flipbook particle effects!

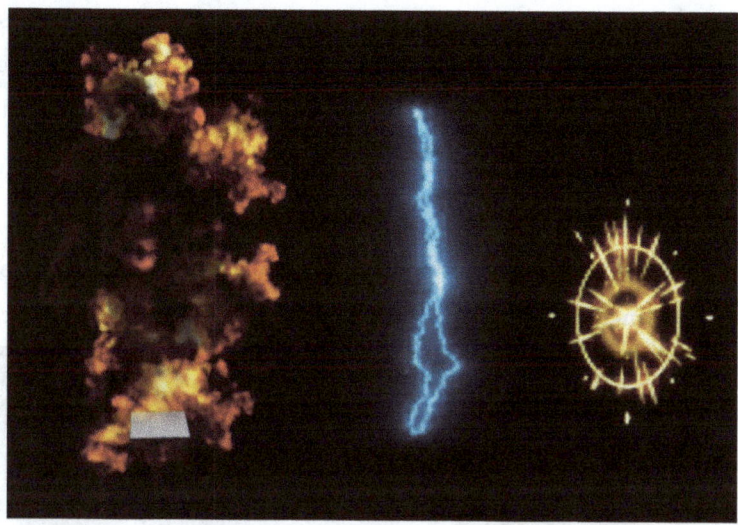

Figure 4.13: Finished flipbook effects

Through this recipe, you have learned how to use **FlipbookLayout** property options within particle emitters. You successfully used a gridded texture to create a base effect and then used your knowledge and creativity to create a realistic flipbook particle. Now, let's move on to the next recipe to see how we can utilize the **Trail** effect.

Trailing behind players

The third available object that we will be going over in this chapter is **Trail**. The **Trail** object is like the beam effect as it has two points, though instead of the beam being statically placed, trails are emitted as the two points move within a space. This makes trails useful when creating things such as footprints, tracers, and moving objects. In this recipe, we will be looking at how to create a trail effect and then make it follow behind the players using a simple script.

How to do it...

We will start by inserting a **Trail** object into a part and then modifying its **Lifetime** and **Color Sequence** values to give it a fun gradient. We will then change the **Max Length** value and the **ImageID** texture. To finish, we will move the trail into the **ServerStorage** object and insert a script into the **ServerScriptService** object. To begin, follow these steps:

1. Insert a **Trail** object into a part in **Workspace**.
2. In the trail's property box, change its **Lifetime** value to 3.6 seconds.
3. Now, open the **Color Sequence** menu by clicking the three dots beside **Color** within the property box. This will open the **Color** pop-up menu.

4. Select the first yellow triangle keyframe at the bottom of the pop-up menu to bring up the color selector, and then choose a color. In this example, I use the `138, 35, 255` color.

5. Next, select the other yellow triangle keyframe and then choose a different color, such as `188, 130, 255`. This will create a gradient effect for our trail.

6. If you want a consistent color, just double-click the color square beside **Color** and it will open the regular color menu.

7. Click **Close** on the **Color Sequence** menu when you've finished selecting the colors.

8. Change the **Max Length** value to `50`. The larger the number, the longer the trail can be:

Figure 4.14: Trail

9. Next, insert one of the following image IDs into the **Texture** box if you want something other than the default trail:

    - `rbxassetid://15289167766`
    - `rbxassetid://15289164328`

10. Now that you're satisfied with the visual look of your trail, we will create a script that will replicate the trail onto the **HumanoidRootPort** object of the player when they join the experience. To do this, move the trail from the part into the **ServerStorage** object. Since the **HumanoidRootPart** object is the center of the avatar, it is the best place to add the trail.

11. In the trail's property box, select the **Attachment0** box and then click the red **X** sign to delete the attachment's parent. Parents are objects that contain other objects. Similarly, children are objects that are contained within a parent.

12. Now, insert a script into the **ServerScriptService** object, or use the *trail script* provided within the `Chapter 4` folder.

13. Open the script by double-clicking it.

14. Paste the following code into your script. With this, you now should have a trail that follows behind players as they move around:

```
game.Players.PlayerAdded:Connect(function(player)
   player.CharacterAdded:Connect(function(char)
      local trail = game.ServerStorage.Trail:Clone()
      trail.Parent = char.Head
      local attachment0 = Instance.new
        ("Attachment",char.Head)
      attachment0.Name = "TrailAttachment0"
      local attachment1 = Instance.new
        ("Attachment",char.HumanoidRootPart)
      attachment1.Name = "TrailAttachment1"
      trail.Attachment0 = attachment0
      trail.Attachment1 = attachment1
   end)
end)
```

Now, you and other players will receive a trail effect when they join the experience, as seen in *Figure 4.15*:

Figure 4.15: Trail following behind the player

With your trail complete, you have now successfully utilized all the available effects provided in Roblox Studio. Through this recipe, you've learned the difference between a trail and a beam, and then skillfully created a trail that follows behind players as they run through the map. Let's now see how we can utilize the rotation properties for particles in the next recipe.

Building a whirlwind

In this recipe, we will be diving further into the customization options of particle effects, specifically with the **EmitterShape** and **Emission** properties. We will be learning how to apply rotation and **SpreadAngle** to give the particles a spin, then modify the **Shape** and **ShapeStyle** properties to get the needed parameters that will allow us to create a fun whirlpool of particles. We will see how we can change the shape of the emitter.

How to do it…

We will start by inserting a **ParticleEmitter** object into a part placed in **Workspace**. Next, we will modify the emitter's **LightEmission** property and then add our own texture. Next, we will change the various parameters of the particles, and finish off by setting the **Orientation** value to **FaceCamera**. To start this recipe, follow these steps:

1. Insert a square part into **Workspace**.
2. Now, insert a **ParticleEmitter** object into the part.
3. Rename the **ParticleEmitter** object `Whirlwind`.
4. Change the particle's **LightEmission** property value to `0.65`.
5. Change the **Texture** value to one of the following image IDs:
   - `rbxassetid://15289228605`
   - `rbxassetid://15289223124`
   - `rbxassetid://15289232756`
6. Change the **ZOffset** value to 3. This will move the render position of the particles forward in front of the emitter part.
7. Set the **Lifetime** value to 3 seconds.
8. Change the **Rate** value to `25`.
9. Now, set the **Rotation** value to `-150`.
10. Change the **RotSpeed** property value to `180`.
11. Set the **Speed** number value to `30`.
12. Next, open the **TransparencySequence** menu and set your desired transparency levels. In this example, I had it fade from `0.15` to `1`.
13. In the **EmitterShape** property tab, change the **Shape** type to `Sphere`. This will cause the particles to emit in the bounding shape of a sphere.
14. Under the same tab, change the **ShapeInOut** option to `Outward` to cause the particles to emit outward.

15. Change the **ShapePartial** number value to 0.02.
16. Set the **ShapeStyle** property value to **Surface**. Changing this property will affect the shape of the particle emission.
17. Change the **Color** value of the particles. In this example, I used the 11, 86, 248 and 109, 218, 248 colors.
18. Now, change the size of the particles by opening the **Size Graph** box. You can see how I set the keyframes in *Figure 4.16*:

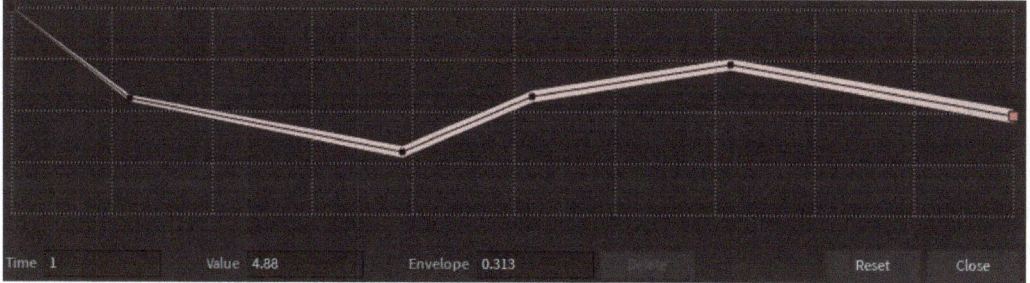

Figure 4.16: Size graph for the particles

19. Set the **Orientation** value to FacingCamera.
20. You can change the direction that the particle blows by enabling wind. You do this by selecting **Workspace** object inside of the Explorer and then setting the values of the **X**, **Y**, and **Z** fields under the **GlobalWind** property.
21. Now, select the particle and enable the **WindAffectsDrag** object in the property box.
22. Finally, change the number inside of the field box. In this example, I'm using a value of 0.15. That concludes the steps to creating a spinning whirlwind like a tornado!

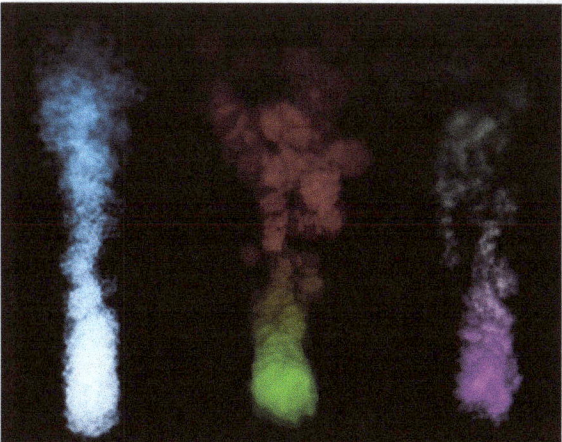

Figure 4.17: Spinning whirlwind variants

You now have a firm grasp on how to make particles vary in shape as well as how to apply rotation to your effects! Let's move on to the final recipe of this chapter where we will learn how to rain particles down from above.

Snowflakes falling from above

In this final recipe, we create a large plane above the ground, which will slowly drop snow down using a **ParticleEmitter** object. Although we're using snowflakes for this example, you can easily swap out the texture for rain, dust, or other things that fall from the sky, or pair it with the cloud that we made in the *Making volumetric smoke with particles* recipe.

How to do it...

We will begin by creating a large flat plane using a transparent part and then moving it upward along its *y* axis. Next, we will insert a **ParticleEmitter** object into the part and modify the **Brightness** and **EmissionDirection** properties. We will then insert our snowflake texture and then finish the recipe by changing the particle emitter's property attributes. To begin, follow these steps:

1. Start by inserting a square part onto the baseplate.
2. Rescale the part to `80, 0.1, 80` studs.
3. Move the part upward along the *y* axis about `55` studs.
4. Turn the part invisible by setting the part's **Transparency** value to `1`.
5. Disable the **CanCollide** box.
6. Disable the **CanTouch** box.
7. Insert a **ParticleEmitter** object into the part.
8. Rename the **ParticleEmitter** object `SnowFall`.
9. In the property box, set the particle's **Brightness** value to `3.185`.
10. Change the **EmissionDirection** property value to `Bottom`.
11. Set the **Lifetime** value to `2, 3`, or however long for the snow to reach the baseplate.
12. Change the **Color** value to white, or the `255, 255, 255` color key.
13. Next, change the **LightEmission** number value to `0`.
14. Change the **LightInfluence** number value to `0`.
15. Now, change the **Size** value of the particles to `0.65`.

16. Insert your snowflake **ImageID** texture into the **Texture** box, or use one of the ones provided here:

    - rbxassetid://12052934252
    - rbxassetid://15289348064
    - rbxassetid://15289347169

17. Open the **Transparency Graph** box and then change the first **Keymark** object's value to 1 and the second **Keymark** object's value to 0.125.

18. Change the **Rate** value to 100. The higher the rate, the more snowflakes there are.

19. Set the **Rotation** value to -25, 25.

20. Now, change the **RotSpeed** property value to -7, 4.

21. Finally, change the **Speed** number value to 25. You now have a particle emitter that falls from above, which is great for snow, rain, and the like:

Figure 4.18: Finished snowfall

That concludes the final recipe of this chapter. Through the course of following the recipes, you have successfully learned how to utilize the default fire, smoke, and sparkle effects. You continued to build your understanding by creating particles, trails, and beams from scratch. Along the way, you've learned how to modify and adjust all the various properties that make up the look and behavior of the particles. Now, let's move on to the next chapter where we will be using our collected knowledge to build an obstacle course.

5
Building a Multiplayer Obby

One of the most popular genres on Roblox since the dawn of the platform has been obbies. *Easy Endless Obby*, *Tower of Hell*, and *Barry's Prison Run* are all obstacle course levels laid out in a mostly linear progression style and feature a winners' room at the end.

In this chapter, we will be constructing an entire obby game, start to finish. This includes building the starting lobby, four unique levels, and the winners' room, and putting it all together with a checkpoint system that saves your progress. Some of these levels have lava, which we will create by inserting a script. There are also spinning objects in many obbies that are made using **CylindricalConstraint**. By the end of this chapter, you will not only have a solid grasp of how to use new plugins such as **Resize Align** and **Archimedes** but also need-to-know knowledge to build an entire obby game, from start to finish.

In this chapter, we're going to cover the following main topics:

- Building the obby lobby
- Creating an obby template
- Creating stage 1 – Slide
- Creating stage 2 – Truss course
- Creating stage 3 – Lava
- Creating stage 4 – Spinning blades
- Building the winners' area
- Setting up respawn checkpoints

Technical requirements

You will need the latest version of Roblox Studio downloaded (at the time of writing, version `1.6.0.50595`).

In this chapter, we will be building out of primitive parts that can be found in the build kit located inside the `Chapter 5` folder at `https://packt.link/gbz/9781805121596`.

You will also need the single script found in the `Chapter 5` folder, which will allow our lava parts to work. Finally, install the **Resize Align** and **Archimedes** plugins, which can be found in the Studio's **Toolbox Plugin** search.

Optionally, you can also download the build kit here: `https://create.roblox.com/marketplace/asset/6579379817/Build-Kit`.

Building the obby lobby

In this recipe, we will be going through the procedure of building the starting spawn lobby. The lobby gives players their first impressions of the game, so we will learn about methods to capture players' attention to keep them engaged by building a stimulating spawn area.

How to do it...

To begin, we will start by creating a hexagon shape for the floor of the lobby. To do so, we will create the shape by rotating square parts into a hexagonal shape, then using the **Resize Align** plugin to connect the edges seamlessly. Next, we will build out the walls, and then create start text with the **ThreeDtext Generator** plugin after we place the player spawns. Lastly, we will build arch pillars over the start, and then use the **Archimedes** plugin to generate an arch. To begin, let's look at the following steps:

1. Insert a square part onto the baseplate, and rescale it to be the length that you want your lobby to be. The thinner the width of the part, the more circular the final shape. In this example, the part is sized `106, 3.5, 28` studs, which will create a dodecagon shape consisting of `10` sides.

2. Duplicate the part and rotate it in increments of `15` degrees past the original. Repeat this step until you have your completed shape:

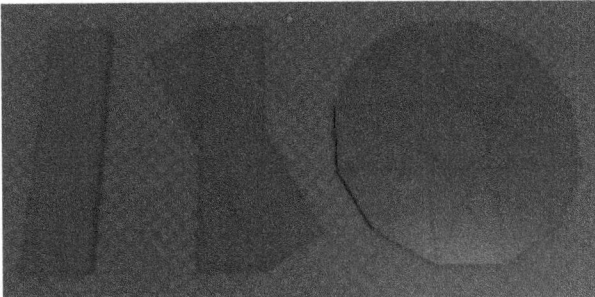

Figure 5.1: Creating a dodecagon shape

3. Group the floor parts together and rename the model `Floor`.
4. Change the floor color to `255, 255, 255` so that it's easier to differentiate parts as we build.
5. Next, click the **Resize Align** plugin, then select two edges to connect them together. Connect all edges together to finish the floor.

6. Now, using square parts, build walls around the perimeter of the floor. In this example, the walls are 3 studs wide and 2.5 studs tall.
7. Select one of the wall parts, duplicate it, then move both parts 25 studs back to create an opening in the wall for where the start line will be.
8. Now, select all the wall parts and group them, then rename the model `Walls`.
9. Select the wall group and duplicate it.
10. Select all the parts inside of the wall group, then use the **Multiple Part Resizer** plugin to increase the height selected of the wall's 0.5 studs. Then, resize the walls from the bottom upward to make these walls sit on top of the original walls. This creates wall caps:

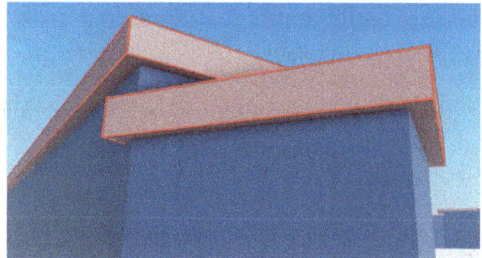

Figure 5.2: Wall cap

11. With the top cap parts still selected, use the **Multiple Part Resizer** plugin and resize the *x* and *z* axes to make the cap overhang the wall by 0.25 studs.
12. Now, insert a cylinder part into the center of your lobby. In this example, the cylinder part is scaled to 0.5, 63, 63 studs.
13. Insert one spawn point from the **Model** tab and place it in the center of the cylinder. Duplicate this spawn point twice, and place each duplicated point on each side of the original spawn point.
14. Open the **ThreeDtext Generator** plugin and click the starting line area. This will prompt you to type your text in, and you can type in START. Customize the text font and then click **Generate** to create the start line text:

Figure 5.3: Text created with the 3Dtext Generator plugin

15. Flip your text 180 degrees so that it's readable from the spawn points.
16. Now, to build an arch over the entrance, add two square parts on each side of the entrance. Resize these parts appropriately so that they look like pillars.
17. Duplicate both parts to create an extruded base for both pillars by enlarging the *x* and *z* axes and shrinking the *y* axis.
18. Using the **Archimedes** plugin, set the **Angle** value to 15 degrees and then click on one of the pillars.
19. Next, set the **Direction** and **Control** settings in **Archimedes** so that when you click **Render**, it will create parts in the shape of a half circle.

    If your arch does not line up to the other side, you may need to resize the part that you're using to create the arch or change the degrees at which it's rotating them.
20. Connect both parts to complete the entrance arch by using the **Resize Align** plugin.
21. Group all the parts in your lobby and rename the model Lobby.
22. Color the parts of your lobby. In this example, I made the floor color 174, 173, 176, the arch and wall color 64, 90, 176, and the wall cap 220, 144, 219.
23. *Optional*: Add material to your lobby. In this example, we are using only smooth plastic and **Neon** material to give it a clean, low-poly feel.

This concludes the first recipe of this chapter, and you can see the completed lobby in *Figure 5.4*:

Figure 5.4: Completed lobby

You should now understand how to use the **Multiple Part Resizer**, **3Dtext Generator**, and **Archimedes** plugins, which are all very powerful tools when it comes to building on Roblox.

Creating the obby template

In this recipe, we will be designing an obby template that we will use for all future stages built in this chapter. This will allow us to create easily connectable and consistently sized courses.

How to do it...

To start this recipe, we will first create a template by scaling a part into a platform to which we will apply an arrow decal. Next, we will create an obby path area that dictates the length of each obby. To begin, follow these steps:

1. To create our template, insert a square part into **Workspace** and scale it to the size of your desired obby. In this example, the part size is `12, 1, 54` studs, and we will refer to it as the obby area, representing the length of the obby.
2. Duplicate this part and attach it to the front. Rescale this part to be `12, 1, 12` studs, which will be our *finishing* platform.
3. Duplicate the finishing platform and move it up `0.1` studs. Downsize the same part `0.5` studs on both the *x* and *z* axes to create another platform.
4. Open **Toolbox** and search for the word `arrow` under the image search, or use the one provided inside the build kit of the `Chapter 5` folder.
5. Paste the decal on top of the newly placed platform. This is our finishing platform. The arrow will point in the direction of the next obby stage. If your arrow is pointing in the wrong direction, select the part that the decal is applied to and rotate it by using *Ctrl* + *R*.
6. Attach a `1x1x1`-stud cube to the opposite side of the obby area, positioned in the center-back. This will be the starting point of the obby.
7. Group all of the parts together and rename the model `ObbyTemplate`.
8. Next, select and then duplicate the template and store the duplicated template inside of the **ServerStorage** object found in the **Explorer** window. This ensures that the original template is not accidentally deleted or modified. You can copy and paste the template over every time you're building an obby to keep them consistently scaled.

That concludes the initial steps for constructing future obbies.

In *Figure 5.5*, you will see how your template should look, depending on your chosen width and length:

Figure 5.5: Completed initial steps

There's more...

The maximum distance distance that a player can jump with the default Roblox gravity is around `13-14` studs.

Creating stage 1 – Slide

In this recipe, we will be creating the first level of our obstacle course. Using the same template that we made in *Creating the obby template* recipe, we will construct a series of vertically gapped parts to create a ladder leading to a slide, which will allow players to slide to the next checkpoint.

How to do it...

To begin, we will start by using a duplicate of the template and building a ladder that rises from the start and leads up to a slide that we will build by placing a part, and then using the **Archimedes** plugin to create a curved shape. After building the walls on each side of the slide, we will then make the slide work by placing an invisible vertical part with its **CanCollide** properties turned off and a trip script inserted. To start, let's look at the following steps:

1. Copy and paste the template that we placed inside of the **ServerStorage** object in *Creating the obby template* recipe into **Workspace**.

2. Rescale the obby path part back toward the start to create a 3x12-stud platform.

Figure 5.6: Completed first obby stage

3. Using the method in the *Creating a ladder* recipe from *Chapter 1*, create a ladder using equally spaced blocks scaled at 1, 1, 12 studs with 1 stud gap in between. In this example, the ladder is 10 rungs high, with a total height of 14 studs.

4. Rescale the top rung outward to create a platform at the top of the ladder for players to stand on. In this example, the platform is 12, 1, 7 studs.

5. Using the **Archimedes** plugin, create a slide shape by selecting the platform part and then using the plugin's options to generate a curve, as seen in *Figure 5.7*:

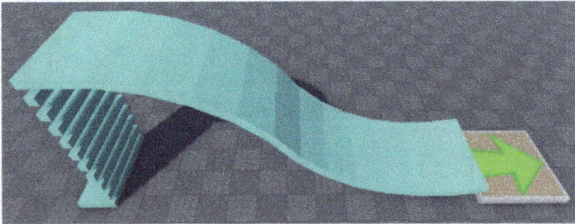

Figure 5.7: Slide shape created

Make sure that your slide curves up at the bottom so that it can launch the players upward onto the finishing platform.

6. Using square parts, add walls to both sides of the slide so that players don't fall off!
7. Use the **Resize Align** plugin to connect the ends of the slide walls.
8. Next, at the top of the slide, place a wide part that the players will walk into.
9. Next, insert the provided **Trip Script,** which can be found in the `Chapter 5` folder, into the part we placed, or insert a script and type the following code:

```
local part = script.Parent
local function onTouched(hit)
    local humanoid = hit.Parent:FindFirstChildWhichIsA('Humanoid')
    if humanoid then humanoid.Sit = true
    end
end

part.Touched:Connect(onTouched)
```

10. Disable the **CanCollide** parts by unchecking the box found in the property box of the seat.
11. Turn the parts' **Transparency** value to `1`.
12. Test your slide to make sure it works and that you can successfully get onto the start platform. If not, you may need to move the finish platform closer or resize the slide. You can test it by clicking the *F5* key on your keyboard or selecting the **Test** option under the **Test** tab found within the Studio top bar.
13. After confirming that your slide works, group and rename the obby `Obby2`.
14. Color your obby to complete the first stage in our course. In this example, I created a rainbow gradient by adjusting the color of each individual part. For example, I started with `220, 110, 185` at the top of the slide, followed by `140, 109, 220`; `104, 145, 220`; `106, 220, 173`; `175, 220, 109`; and `220, 158, 104`. *Figure 5.8* shows what the completed slide obby will look like:

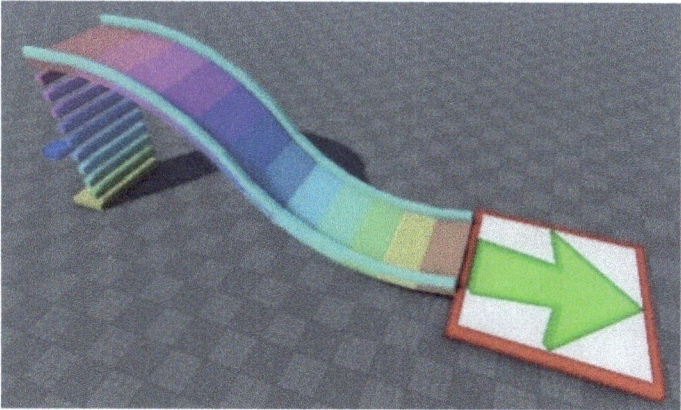

Figure 5.8: Completed slide obby

You now have the knowledge to make a simple slide using a seat part to trip players. You also now know how to test your game within Roblox Studio, which will allow you to make sure all your courses work as you build them through the remainder of the chapter.

Creating stage 2 – Truss course

In this recipe, we will be creating the second stage of the course, which consists of trusses. As we learned in the *Creating a ladder* recipe of *Chapter 1*, trusses are a type of default part that players can climb on. By creating a course using these rather than a traditional part, everything the player touches will essentially be climbable. We will set a part of the stage up to where players must jump from an edge onto a flat wall of trusses to climb onto the next checkpoint.

How to do it...

To begin this recipe, we will start by creating a path of three trusses for the player to walk on that lead to a set of vertical trusses, followed by a row of horizontal trusses. This creates an oversized step. We will then create a maze of trusses leading to the other side toward the finish checkpoint. We will finish by applying color to the trusses. Let's look at the steps now:

1. Copy and paste the obby template into **Workspace**.
2. Delete the obby path part.
3. Move the finish platform `16` studs upward.
4. Insert a **Truss** part from either **Toolbox** or the build kit and place it in the center of the start point.
5. Duplicate the truss twice and move each over 2 studs, making the path three trusses wide.
6. Select all three trusses and use the **Multiple Part Resizer** plugin to make them about 8 studs long.
7. Duplicate the three trusses and place them vertically at the end of the truss path to create a ladder upward.
8. Duplicate the three trusses again and place them horizontally on the top of the truss ladder to create a large step.
9. Duplicate one of the trusses and place it vertically in the center at the end of the horizontal trusses.
10. Using trusses, attach them from the top of the vertical truss we just placed and create a maze path with the trusses.
11. Finish the maze at the center point of the finish platform.
12. Group and rename the model `Obby3`.
13. Recolor the trusses to complete your second obby:

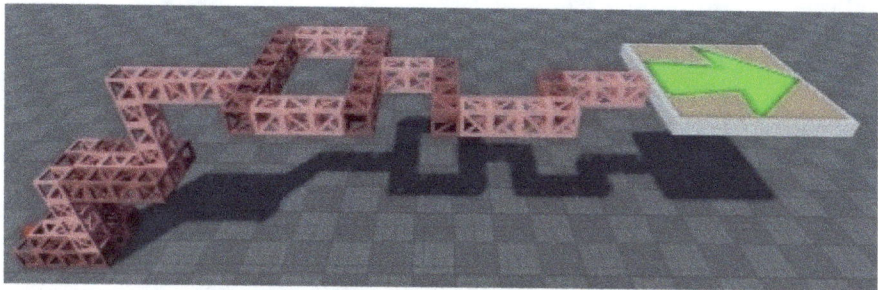

Figure 5.9: Completed second obby built with trusses

You now have a solid understanding of how you can incorporate trusses to create a climbable course.

Creating stage 3 – Lava

In the following recipe, we will be creating the third stage of our course, which contains lava bricks. These lava bricks will respawn the player if they touch them. By placing these bricks through this level, it will make for a fun and challenging level.

How to do it...

To begin this recipe, we will start by creating a path leading from the start platform all the way to the end platform. Next, we will create a lava brick by changing the part's **Material** property to **Neon** and inserting a script into the part. We will then place them throughout the course, creating a maze. To start, follow these steps:

1. Copy and paste the obby template into **Workspace**.
2. Resize the obby path part to 3 studs long, and place it past and flush with the start part.
3. Duplicate this new obby path part, and place it before and flush with the finishing platform.
4. Insert a square part that is `4, 0.5, 4` studs large.
5. Change the part's **Material** property to **Neon**.
6. Change the part's **Color** property, ensuring you use a shade that does not overly bloom – in this example, the color used is `165, 95, 45`. This will be our lava part.
7. Now, insert **Lava Script** found inside the `Chapter 5` folder into the lava brick.
8. Now, create a checker pattern with the lava by placing the lava part on one of the starting corners of the obby path part.
9. Duplicate the lava part and move it 4 studs over, then duplicate that part and move it over another 4 studs so that you have three lava parts side by side.

10. Move the middle lava part up 4 studs:

Figure 5.10: Creating a lava pattern

11. Select the three lava parts and duplicate them.

12. Move the duplicated parts forward 8 studs. Continue to repeat *steps 8* and *9* until you have created a checker pattern across the obby area.

13. Color the base part under the lava. In this example, the color I'm using is 202, 71, 59.

14. Select all the parts and group them together, then rename the model Obby3. This completes the third stage of our obby, where you learned how to apply lava to the course in a checkerboard pattern:

Figure 5.11: Completed third obby

Creating stage 4 – Spinning blades

In this recipe, we will be working with the **CylindricalConstraint** object to build the fourth obstacle stage. The **CylindricalConstraint** object will allow us to rotate a part, creating a spinning motion at our desired speed. This mechanism will allow us to build a unique stage without the need for scripts.

How to do it...

To start, we will create a simple stage out of square and cylinder parts. We will then place a small square part and attach a **CylindricalConstraint** object to it. Next, we will attach blades to the motor and add them to an arm that we created attached to the level path. Finally, we will create a gap so that the spinning blade does not get stuck. To begin your next obby, follow these steps:

1. Copy and paste the obby template into **Workspace**.

2. Resize the obby path part to be 5 studs wide.

3. Using a square part, create an arm attaching from the obby path part out of 5 studs.
4. Select the arm part, then copy and paste it vertically at the end of the first arm part and make it 11 studs tall:

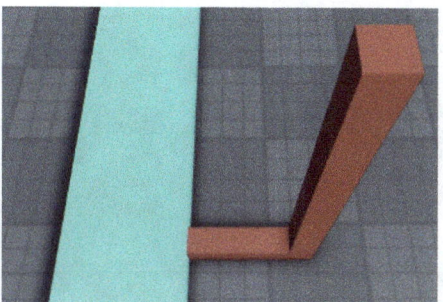

Figure 5.12: Vertical arm

5. Insert a square part and scale it to 2, 1, 2 studs.
6. Select the square part and name the part Base.
7. Duplicate the base, move it up 3 studs, and scale it to be 24 studs long. This will be the spinning blade.
8. Rename the spinning blade Blade.
9. Insert a **CylindricalConstraint** object by selecting it under the **Create Constraint** drop-down menu located within the **Model** tab of the top bar, then click both the top of the base part and underneath the blade.
10. Lower the blade so that it sits on top of the base part.
11. Select both the base and the blade and group them together.
12. Rename the model Spinne 15.
13. Unanchor the blade part.
14. Change the **AngularActuatorType** to **Motor**.
15. You can change how fast the blade spins by changing the **AngularVelocity** property in the **CylindricalConstraint** part. In this example, it is set to -1.5
16. To quickly run your game to check the speed of the blades, you can go to the **Test** tab in the top bar and select **Run**. This will allow the game to run without it spawning in your avatar, making it quicker to test. Click **Stop** in the same spot as the **Run** button once you're finished testing.
17. If you want to turn the spinning blade part into lava, you can insert the lava script used in the previous recipe and then disable the blade's collisions by unchecking the **CanCollide** box. This is so that the blade does not collide with the platform and get stuck. If you want a blade that collides with players, skip this step.

18. Duplicate the obby path and then create a gap where the blade will rotate through. This gap needs to be small enough that players can still jump to the other side 19.

19. Attach the spinner model to the arm:

Figure 5.13: Spinner attached to arm

20. Color the parts of your obby. In this example, I used `142, 202, 190` for the path color and `148, 71, 68` for the other parts.

21. Group all the parts and rename the model `Obby4`. Congratulations! You've just completed your fourth obby!

This concludes the fourth style of obstacle course for our game:

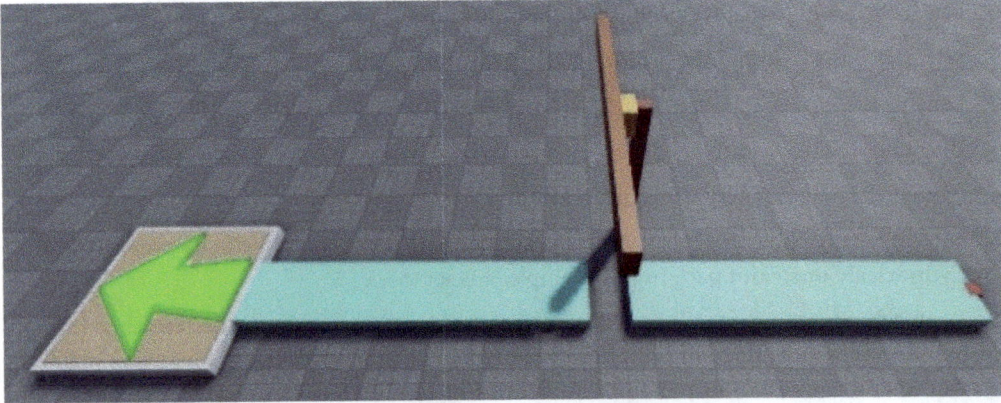

Figure 5.14: Completed fourth obby with a spinning blade

You can now go through and test all your obstacle courses to confirm they work. You now know how to make a variety of different levels with unique mechanics such as spinning blades and lava. Let's see how we can put it all together.

Building the winners' area

In this recipe, we will be building the winners' area at the end of the obby. The winners' room is what is referred to as the "hook" of the game. It offers rewards for players who played through until the end, meaning more players will stay to the end if there is some sort of reward.

How to do it...

To begin, we will build a checker pattern finish line on a platform. Next, we will create a large hexagonal floor using square and wedge parts, then we will decorate it with a neon border. We will then copy and paste the lobby arch we made earlier, and scale it to fit over the checkerboard pattern to indicate the finish. Following that, we will use the **3Dtext Generator** plugin to create winners' text and fit it onto the front of the arch. Finally, we will place gear givers, which are provided in the build kit of the `Chapter 5` folder. To begin, follow these steps:

1. First, copy and paste a finish pad, then attach a `12, 1, 6`-stud part to the end of it to create a platform.
2. Next, insert another part sized to `3, 0.25, 3` and tile it over top of the platform.
3. Recolor the parts into a checker pattern. I used the `197, 190, 190` and `35, 34, 34` colors.
4. Copy and paste the platform that we placed the checker tiles on and place it on the end of the original platform, then rescale it to the size of the winners' room. The part should be around the size of the lobby – enough to have all players standing on it at once without it being crowded. In this example, the part is `40, 1, 50` studs.
5. Duplicate the part and resize it on the *z* axis `10` studs inward both ways.
6. Select the original floor part and resize it on the *x* axis 6 studs inward both ways. This should create a + shape:

Figure 5.15: Plus-shaped floor

7. Next, fill each corner of the floor with `6`, `1`, `6`-stud wedge parts.
8. Add parts with the **Neon** material along the width of the floor on all sides around the perimeter.
9. Select the **Resize Align** plugin, then click two neon faces to connect them. Connect all the neon parts around the parameter together.
10. Using **Toolbox**, or the tools provided inside of the `Chapter 5` folder, place the provided gear givers along the floor against the two longer walls.
11. Copy and paste the arch we built for the lobby onto the winners' floor, and rescale it to fit the opening.
12. Using the **3Dtext Generator** plugin, create text that says `WINNERS`.
13. Place the winners' text at the front of the arch, bending each letter to the curve.

This completes the final step for the winners' room:

Figure 5.16: Completed winners' room

Now, to hook it all up together, we will look at the following recipe.

Setting up respawn checkpoints

In this recipe, we will attach all of our courses together to our lobby and winners' room, then use **Spawn Locations** to allow players to keep their last saved checkpoint even after they reset or fall off the course.

How to do it...

To start, we will connect the first obby to the start area of the lobby. We will then connect the following four obbies, followed by attaching the winners' room at the end of the fourth obby. We will then insert a spawn location from the top bar of the Studio and place it on the first stage's start platform. Next, we'll set up the properties so that we can then copy and paste the spawn location onto all the other platforms. Finally, we will modify the properties of each spawn individually to assign them their own name and checkpoint color. To begin this recipe, let's look at the following steps:

1. Start by connecting the obbies together with the starter lobby at the start and the winners' area at the back.
2. Now, insert a spawn location from the **Model** tab of the top bar and place it on the first obby's finish platform.
3. Delete the spawn's decal and make the part's **Transparency** value 1.
4. Disable collisions on the spawn by unchecking the **CanCollide** property box.
5. In the **Team** dropdown of the property box, uncheck the **Neutral** property so that players don't spawn on this by default when they join the game, then enable **AllowTeamChangeOnTouch**. Players will now spawn on this checkpoint as long as they touch the spawn location part before respawning.
6. Copy and paste the spawn onto every obby's finish platform and on the checker pattern of the winners' room.
7. Change each of the spawns' **TeamColor** property to a different color.

This completes the final recipe of this chapter:

Figure 5.17: Finished obby

You now have a deep understanding of how to create multiple styles of obstacle courses using spaced blocks, lava bricks, slides, and spinning blades. You have also learned how to create both a spawn lobby as well as a winners' room at the end, meaning you now have a fully functioning obby game ready to be published!

6
Designing a House

In this chapter, we will be using our gathered knowledge of building with primitive parts and plugins to construct a full house with a furnished interior. Through this chapter, we will be following a basic workflow method that works when creating any building.

We will start by creating a floor plan on top of our house's foundation using parts and labeling it using the **3Dtext** plugin. We will build the walls and learn the value of grayboxing as we block out the future placement of props. We will then illuminate the interior of the house using volumetric lighting, create a roof, and finish the house off by replacing our grayboxed props with their final assets.

Now, put on your hard hat, and let's head into Roblox Studio!

In this chapter, we're going to cover the following main topics:

- Blueprinting your house
- Building out the walls
- Adding windows, doors, and floors
- Grayboxing the props
- Adding lights and ceilings
- Creating a roof and front overhang
- Finalizing your house

Technical requirements

You will need the latest version of Roblox Studio downloaded (at the time of writing, version *1.6.0.50595*).

In this chapter, we will be filling the house with furniture props, which can be found inside the Chapter 6 folder at https://packt.link/gbz/9781805121596.

The **Prop Pack** can be found here: `https://www.roblox.com/library/14853000092`. You will also need the **Resize Align** and **3Dtext** plugins, which can be found in the Studio **Toolbox Plugin** search.

Blueprinting your house

In this recipe, we will be using our knowledge of building with primitive parts to block out and create a laid-out foundation for our house to sit on. We will use the **3Dtext** plugin to label each of the rooms and create a sidewalk leading from the entrance to a roadway.

How to do it...

We will start by unlocking the baseplate and then resizing it. We will continue by creating a sidewalk and roadway with dotted lines to indicate the front of the home. Next, we will create the foundation shape and size, then split the foundation up into rooms by placing differently colored parts on top and then labeling them with the **ThreeDtext** plugin. We will finish the recipe by creating a sidewalk leading from the front entrance to the roadway. To begin, follow these steps:

1. First, select the baseplate by either selecting it in **Workspace** or by unlocking it with the **Lock** tool (*Alt + L*).
2. Next, resize the baseplate to `100, 1, 100` studs.
3. Change the baseplate color to `75, 151, 75` to represent the grass plot for the house.
4. Change the grass part material to `Grass`.
5. Stretch a `6.75`-stud-wide part – colored to `133, 132, 135` – across one of the sides of the plot as a sidewalk.
6. Scale the sidewalk so that it's extruding `0.25` studs above the grass.
7. Create a roadway using a part colored `10, 10, 10` on one side of the plot to indicate the front of the house.
8. Create some dotted traffic lines by placing `0.5, 0.05, 5.15`-sized parts on the road and spacing them `15` studs from each other. Color these parts to `255, 255, 0`.
9. Next, add a thin line along the entire length of the road 1 stud away from the sidewalk. Color this part to `255, 255, 255`.
10. Next, insert a square part in the center of the grass plot and scale it to the desired size of your house. In this recipe, the part size is `53, 1, 69` studs. This will be the house foundation.
11. Now, duplicate the sidewalk and rotate it `90` degrees.
12. Place the duplicated sidewalk part on the foundation where you want your front entrance to be.

13. Resize the duplicated sidewalk to fit against the original sidewalk part.
14. Next, lay out the rooms for the house on top of the foundation using flat parts.
15. Recolor each of the room parts with a different color to help differentiate them from one another. The colors used in this example are `164, 189, 71`, `123, 47, 123`, and `77, 147, 139`.
16. Using the **ThreeDtext Generator** plugin, add a text label to each room (such as kitchen, bedroom, and so on).

You now have your house plot and laid-out foundation all complete and ready to further lay out with walls, which we will be doing in the *Building out the walls* recipe:

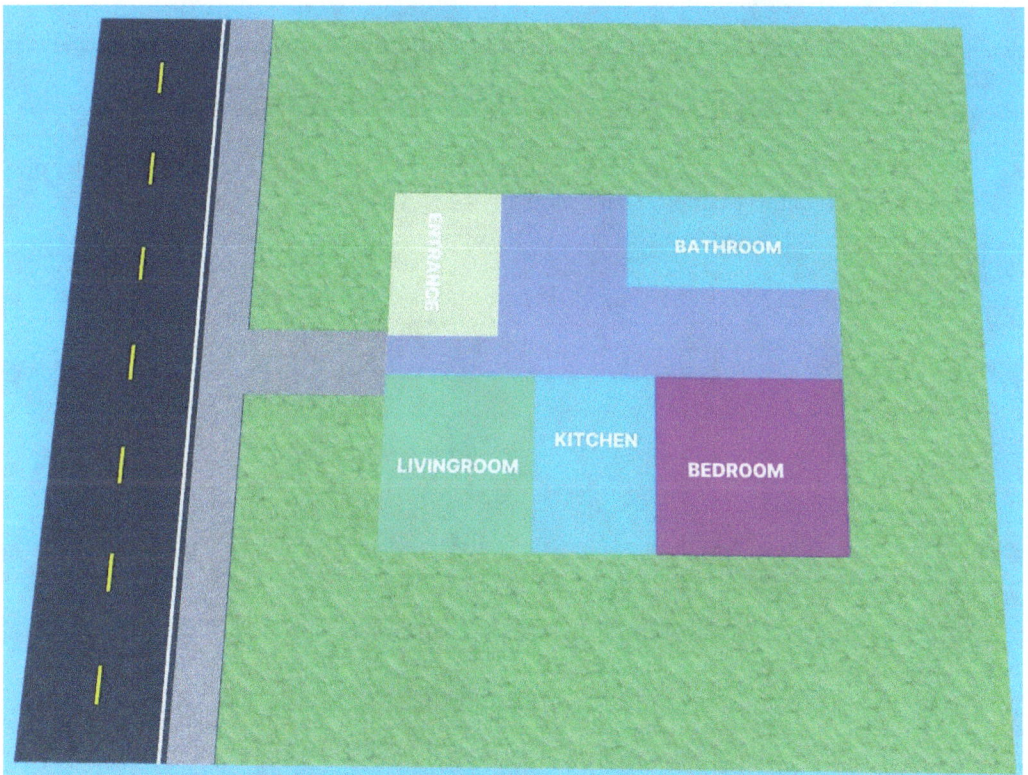

Figure 6.1: Finished 3D blueprint

Building out the walls

In this recipe, we will be further building out the house by adding parts to represent the doors and windows of the house. We will then be building out both the exterior and interior walls and finishing up by creating a baseboard and top board along the top of the walls. Let's see how we can do this next.

How to do it...

To begin, we will create a door reference part and paste it throughout the house to indicate where doorways will be. Next, we will place a different colored part around the perimiter of the foundation walls to represent the windows. We will then build out the exterior walls, followed by building the interior walls around our labeled room parts. To finish, we will be adding baseboard and top board to the interior walls. To begin, follow these steps:

1. Start by placing a part to represent the front entrance's door. The door part used in this recipe scale is `6, 8, 0.5` studs. This door part will be used as a reference to help keep all the doorways scaled consistently.

2. Now, duplicate the door part and place it at the back of the house foundation to represent the back doorway.

3. Next, duplicate the door part again and place a door part in each room.

4. Next, place a different colored part representing the windows around the outer perimeter of the foundation. In this example, I used the `12, 41, 147` color:

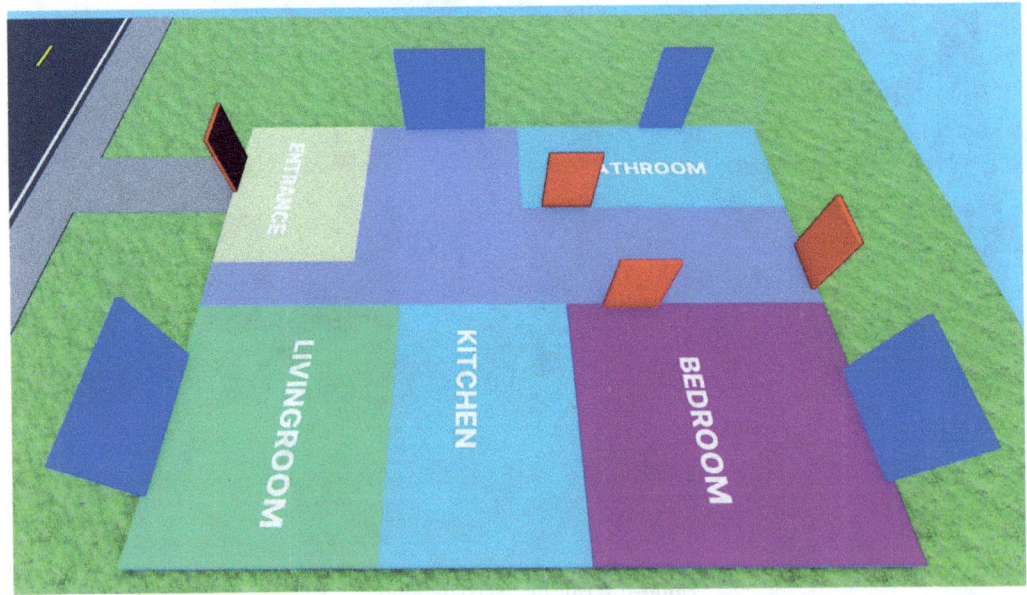

Figure 6.2: Windows and door reference parts

5. Now, using a `0.5 x 13.5`-stud-tall part, add exterior walls along the perimeter of your house.

6. Next, using the same thickness part, build the interior walls around each room and doorway:

Figure 6.3: Interior walls added

7. Group your interior walls together. Remember to continue to group and name similar objects together to stay organized.

8. Now, add a `0.05`-stud-thin part to the inside walls of the bedroom. This will work like wallpaper and allow us to apply different colors to each of the rooms:

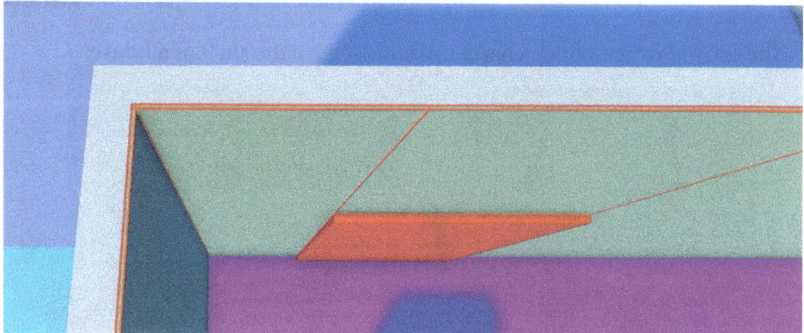

Figure 6.4: Wallpaper

9. Group the wallpaper parts together and rename the model `WallpaperBedroom_01`. This will help keep your **Workspace** clean and the models organized.

10. Change the color of the wallpaper parts – for example, `147, 130, 118`, `93, 147, 122`, or `204, 175, 216`.

11. Repeat *steps 8–10* for all interior rooms of the house. You should have each room's wall filled with wallpaper broken up into named models; that is, `WallpaperBathroom_01`, `WallpaperBedroom_01`, `WallpaperKitchen_01`, and so on.

108   Designing a House

12. Next, insert a square part into **Workspace** and scale it to `2, 0.4, 0.15` studs.

13. Place the part onto the bottom of one of the interior walls and rescale it the entirety of the wall's length. This will leave you with a thin part along the base of the wall.

14. Duplicate the part and create an outline along the bottom of all the interior walls. Once you're finished with placing the parts, make sure you group them into a single model. This will be the house's baseboard:

Figure 6.5: Baseboard along the bottom of the walls

15. Now, like how we placed the baseboard previously in *steps 12–14*, create an outline along the top of the walls with a part scaled 2 studs wide and 1 stud tall. This will be our wall's top board and will help the room feel as if it has a lot more depth, versus having just bland, flat walls.

This completes the second recipe of this chapter. You now have the shell of a house:

Figure 6.6: Finished walls

Let's see how we can continue to build our home with the next recipe.

There's more...

Make sure to consider the players' perspective when building your wall height. Give the player a lot of headroom to ensure that they have room to maneuver their camera. In this recipe, we used a ceiling height of `13.5` studs, which gives a good amount of room to move the camera.

Adding windows, doors, and floors

In this recipe, we will be applying flooring in the house with various textures in each room. We will then be building out the door frames of the house and connecting them to the baseboard. We will finish the recipe by creating window frames and adding glass to the frames. Let's see how we can do this next.

How to do it...

To start, we will be deleting the room layout parts and text as well as the parts representing the windows and doorways. We will then apply parts with textures onto the floors throughout the house and add floor stops in the doorways to help create cleaner transitions between floor styles. We will then add the door frames using square parts, and then in a similar fashion add frames to the window spaces. We will finish the windows and recipe by adding inner window frames and glass. To begin, follow these steps:

1. Start by deleting the room layout parts and text that we created in the *Blueprinting your house* recipe so that only the foundation remains. Alternatively, you can keep the room layout parts and rescale them for this recipe.
2. Now, delete the window and doorway parts that we placed while creating the layout in the *Building out the walls* recipe.
3. Next, insert a square part onto the floor in the room and flatten it to be `0.1` studs tall, then place it onto the floor of the bedroom.
4. Rescale the square part to fit the floor dimensions of the room.
5. Add a thin part in the middle of the doorway and make sure the bedroom's floor is flush with it to work as a floor divider, making the transitions between floor textures more seamless.
6. Repeat *steps 1-5* in every room of the house so that the entire house's floor space is covered with parts fitted to each room, and every doorway has a floor divider part.
7. Now, right-click on one of the floor parts and insert a `Texture` object. Set the texture's **Face** direction so that the texture sits on top of the part.
8. Copy and paste the texture onto the top of each room's floor part.
9. Change the image IDs of the textures to your desired image ID. The IDs used in this recipe are as listed:

    Living room hardwood: `10990326093`

    Bathroom tile: `6794252529`

Bedroom carpet: 11316012316

Entrance carpet: 2718728195

Figure 6.7 shows how your floor textures should vary to help identify different rooms:

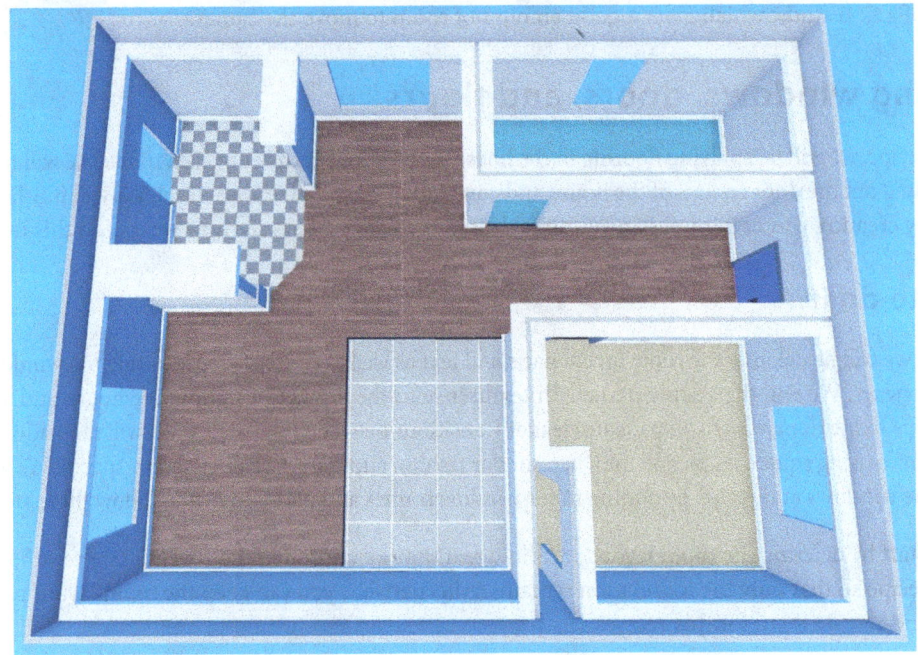

Figure 6.7: Finished floors

10. If a room's floor has more than two parts, the textures may not align with each other. There are the following two fixes for this:

    - The first is the proper way. Select a texture, and inside of the property box, adjust the values of the **StudOffsetU** and **StudOffsetV** fields until the textures align.

    - Alternatively, you can select the parts inside of the room and union them together.

11. Now, create a door frame using three square parts, as seen in *Figure 6.8*. The door frame parts in this example are 8, 0.5, 1 for the sides and 5.5, 0.5, 1 for the top part:

Adding windows, doors, and floors   111

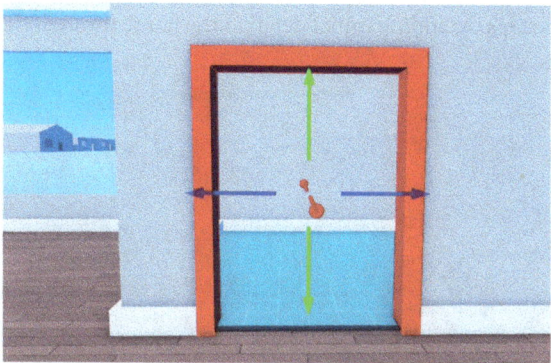

Figure 6.8: Door frame

12. Select the door frame parts and group them together.
13. Rename the door frame model `DoorFrame`.
14. Copy and paste the door frame model into all the doorways.
15. Next, we will build a frame around the four sides of each window using the same method used for the doorways.
16. Insert a part into the center of a window and rescale it to the window's dimensions. This will be the window glass.
17. Change the glass part's **Transparency** value to `0.6`.
18. Disable the glass part's **CastShadow** property.
19. Change the part's **Color** value to `13, 105, 172`.
20. Rename the part `Glass`.
21. Create a T-shape frame inside of the window using thinner parts than the window frame. Your window should look similar to the following figure:

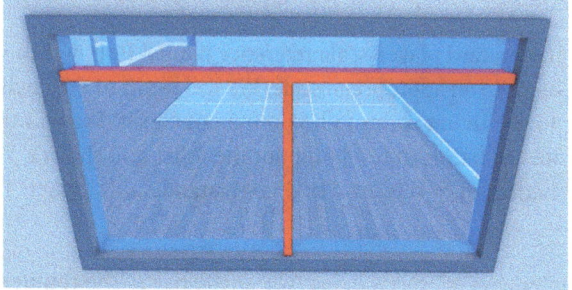

Figure 6.9: Completed window

22. Copy and paste the glass and T-frame into the other window frames.

This completes this recipe's steps on adding initial detail to the home through the addition of flooring, windows, and door frames:

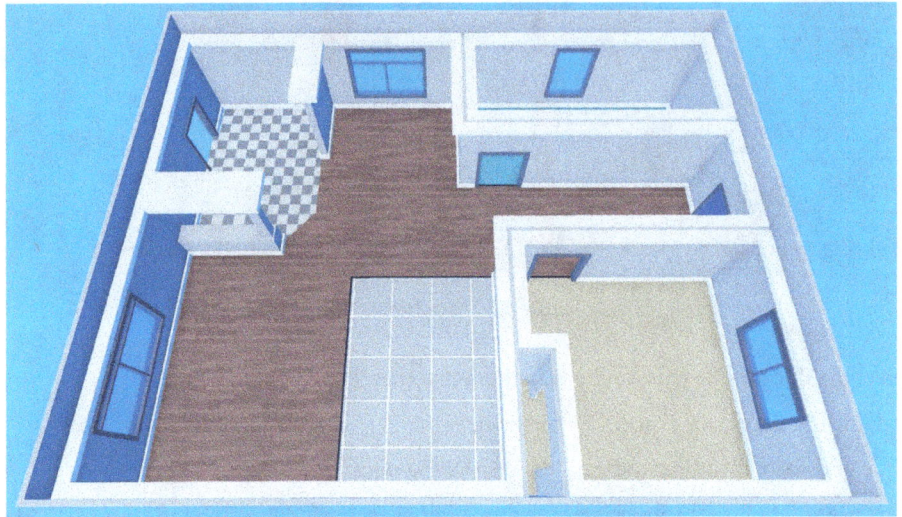

Figure 6.10: Windows, floor, and doorways

Grayboxing the props

In this recipe, we will be going from room to room creating very simple silhouettes of props that we will be adding later in the *Finalizing your house* recipe. This is called **grayboxing**, which means to create very simple shapes that help give us an idea of which prop will go where. Grayboxing is a very useful step to ensure that you have a clear vision of what your map will look like before spending an excessive amount of time creating the final assets.

How to do it...

To begin, we will insert the standard player-scale reference named **Bob**, which we will use to ensure that we are building each room to an appropriate scale. We will begin in the kitchen creating counters and an island, then over to the living room to box out a couch set. We will then create a kitchen table set before moving into the bathroom to build out the toilet and shower. We will finish off this recipe by grayboxing the bedroom by adding a bed, nightstand, and dresser. To begin, let's look at the following steps:

1. Create kitchen counters in an L shape using two square parts. The counters in this example are scaled 2.5 studs tall and 2.5 studs wide.
2. Duplicate the L-shaped counters and move them upward, just below the ceiling, to create upper cabinets.

3. Next, build a sink and faucet on one of the L-shape countertops. Remember – the graybox does not need to be detailed. You can read more about grayboxing in the *There's more...* section at the end of this recipe.
4. Build a fridge beside the counters, and a microwave on top of the counter using square parts to create the primitive shape of the object.
5. Next, create a kitchen island in the middle of the room using a rectangular part:

Figure 6.11: Finished kitchen graybox

6. In the middle of the living room floor facing one of the walls, create the shape of a couch.
7. Next, build out the shape of a coffee table in front of the couch.
8. Now, build a TV mounted onto the wall and a lamp in the corner beside it.
9. Beside the kitchen area, create a table and chair dinner table set, and a clock on the wall.
10. Against the back wall of the kitchen area, create a potted plant.
11. Moving into the bathroom, create the shape of a toilet using square parts.
12. Now, create either a shower, bathtub, or both!
13. Build the bathroom sink cabinet with a sink built into the top.
14. Add a part onto the wall in front of the sink and change its **Reflectance** property to 0.75 to create a mirror.
15. Create a tall cabinet shelf for towels against one of the bathroom walls. We can see in *Figure 6.12* how the bathroom is beginning to take shape, even with the simplicity of the graybox:

Figure 6.12: Top-down view of the bathroom graybox

16. Now, build a shoe rack and shelf by the back entrance area of the house.
17. Now, duplicate the shoe rack to the front entrance's door.
18. Create a hat rack by the front entrance.
19. In the bedroom, build a bed and a nightstand beside it. Then, build a TV stand with a TV on top and place it against the wall in front of the bed.
20. Finally, create a tall dresser cabinet against an empty wall of the bedroom.

This concludes the steps for grayboxing the interior of the house:

Figure 6.13: Grayboxed props fill the house

Let's now look at the next recipe to see how we can continue to evolve the design.

There's more...

Grayboxing, also known as grayscaling or a blockout, is not meant to be detailed. It is meant to create a general rough draft of the room before it gets replaced with a polished asset. Grayboxing is great on both large and small maps because it allows you to create a simplified level that you can test and scale according to. This is much better than creating a bunch of assets just to realize that they don't fit your level.

Adding lights and ceilings

In this recipe, we will be creating a ceiling in each room of the house. We will decorate the ceiling with pot light fixtures that we will build, as well as create a neon strip around the top board of the bedroom ceiling. We will finish off the recipe by adding a surface light into a part and using it to project volumetric light into our home.

How to do it...

To start this recipe, we will create a thin part that we will apply at the top of all the rooms to create ceilings. We will then build a single pot light fixture using a neon cylinder part stacked on top of a larger non-neon cylinder. We will add pot lights onto every room's ceiling except the bedroom, where instead we will create a neon strip around the perimeter of the ceiling. To finish, we will create a surface light source by inserting it into an invisible part and then applying it over the top of each room. To begin, follow these steps:

1. Start by adding a `0.25`-stud-thick part across the ceiling of the bedroom, flush with the top board that we created in *step 15* of the *Building out the walls* recipe.
2. Add ceiling parts to all the other rooms of the house.
3. Next, insert a circular part and scale it to `1, 0.2, 1`.
4. Duplicate the part on top of itself, then scale it flat.
5. Rescale the duplicated part inward on the *x* and *z* axis to `0.3` studs.
6. Change the duplicated part's **Material** type to **neon**.
7. Recolor the neon part's color to a warm tone, such as `172, 166, 142`.
8. Select both parts and group them together.
9. Rename the model `LightFixture`:

Figure 6.14: Finished ceiling light fixture

10. Place the light fixture in the ceilings of every room – except the bedroom – with the neon part facing downward.
11. In the bedroom, insert a square part and change its **Material** type to **neon**.
12. Rescale the neon parts to `.2, .2, 4`.
13. Add the neon part along the entire perimeter of the ceiling along the top board of the bedroom:

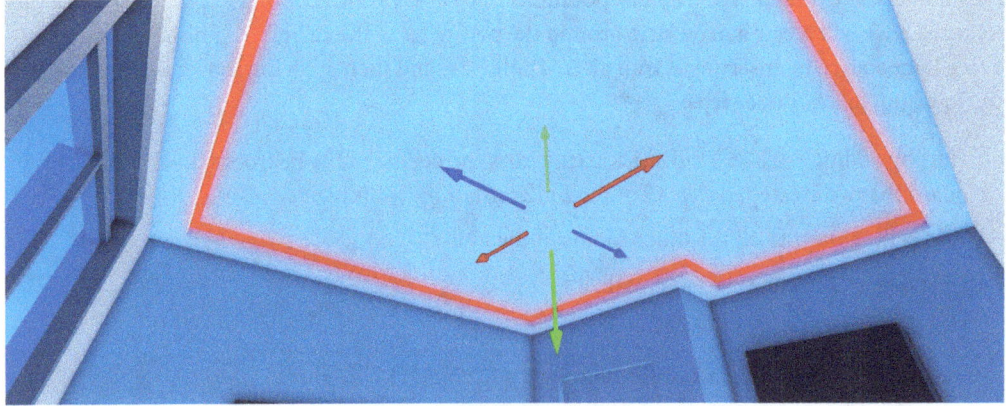

Figure 6.15: Neon outline along ceiling

14. Now, to add volumetric lighting, select the ceiling part in the bedroom and duplicate it.
15. Move the part down the *y* axis so that it fits underneath the original ceiling part. Rescale the part to ensure that it is roughly the same width and length dimensions as the room.
16. Insert a **Surface Light** object into the part that we just resized.
17. Change the part's **Transparency** value to `1`.
18. Uncheck the **CanCollide** box within the part's properties window.

19. Select the surface light object inside of the part and make sure that the light is projecting downward from the correct face.
20. Change the light **Range** value to about 30. You may need more or less range depending on your ceiling height and how far the light needs to project down.
21. Recolor the light to the same color as the light fixture's neon. In this case, it's 172, 166, 142.
22. Duplicate the surface light part into the remaining rooms of the house to finish illuminating the interior.

That completes this recipe. You now have a ceiling as well as light fixtures, and lighting applied across your house:

Figure 6.16: Finished ceiling

There's more...

As there are very few natural light sources being emitted in an indoor environment such as a house, it's good to disable the **CastShadow** property of your interior models and props so that they do not cast unnatural shadows indoors. You can also disable the **CastShadow** property of the ceiling parts to brighten up the room without the need for a volumetric light source, and it also cuts back on the amount needed to light up a room.

Creating a roof and front overhang

In this recipe, we will be constructing a front porch and overhang, as well as the roof for our house using wedge parts. We will detail the roof by adding a top part that overhangs the walls, fascia, and ridge cap.

Designing a House

How to do it...

To begin, we will find the center point of the house, and then use wedge parts to create a roof and desired pitch. We will then create a front porch with an overhanging roof over the top of the front entrance of the house with pillars that hold the overhang up. Next, we will detail the roof by attaching a flat part overhanging the walls and attaching a facia to it. We will finish the roof by applying a roof cap along the roof's peak and then building two roof vents. To begin, follow these steps:

1. Place a brightly colored part along the top center of your house's walls to create a visible line indicating the center of the house. I like to use bright red or green so that the line is clearly visible as I build.

2. Next, place a wedge part on one of the sides on top of the roof and then scale it to connect with the center reference part that we placed previously in *step 1*. Duplicate the wedge part, rotate it `180` degrees, and move it onto the other side to create a sloped roof. Delete the center reference part, then connect the wedges together.

3. Resize both wedges upward along the *y* axis to your desired roof pitch. In this example, the wedges are `8.5` studs tall.

4. Next, add a square part above the doorway to the scale you would like your porch overhang to be. The part in this example is scaled to `29.25, 75, 0.5` studs and is placed over the top of the front entrance door.

5. Create pillars connecting the overhang to the ground, as seen in the following figure:

Figure 6.17: Overhang with pillars

6. Create a sloped roof by inserting two wedge parts on top of the part that we placed above the doorway, the same as we did in *step 2* earlier.

7. Scale up the wedges to your desired pitch. In this example, they are 6 studs tall.
8. Now, add 0.5 tall parts across the top surface of each wedge part, both on the roof and on the overhang. There should be four wedges in total.
9. Resize the parts to overhang each side of the roof by 2 studs.
10. To add a facia, insert a 0.25 x 0.75-stud part along the side faces of the parts we just overhung. The part should be flush at the top, and overhang the bottom by 0.25 studs.
11. Use the **Resize Align** plugin to connect the ends of all the facia together, cleanly.
12. Now, add a 0.5 x 0.5-stud part along the entire length of the rooftops where both roof parts connect. This will create a roof cap that will tie the roof together visually.
13. Add two circular parts to the rooftop. This will create attic exhaust vents.

This completes the last step of this recipe on building a roof. Your house should now have a nicely sloped overhang over the door entrance, as well as a roof fitted on top of your house with a facia and roof cap:

Figure 6.18: Completed roof

Finalizing your house

In this recipe, we will be using long part strips rotated and then stacked above one another to create vinyl siding for the house, then capping it off by adding corner posts. We will then be replacing our grayboxed props with their final assets. We will conclude the recipe and chapter by creating and inserting doors to the open doorways. Let's look at the steps to finish building your house next.

How to do it...

We will start by adding a long part along one of the exterior walls and rotating it 15 degrees. We will then duplicate it and stack the duplicated parts on top of one another until the wall is covered, where we will then cut out the windows and doors. We will finish the siding by adding posts to all four corners of the house. Next, we will replace the existing grayboxed props with their final assets, and then finish the recipe off by creating a door that we will place in all the open doorways. To begin, follow these steps:

1. Place a 1.5-stud-tall x 0.35-stud-thick part along the bottom of one of the exterior walls stretching the entire wall length. This will be our exterior vinyl siding on the home.
2. Rotate the part 10 degrees.
3. Duplicate the part and move it up 0.9 studs along the *y* axis. Repeat this step until the wall is covered with vinyl planks.
4. If your vinyl planks are covering a window or door, cut them out by duplicating the plank, then resizing both parts to sit on each end of the window or door frame:

Figure 6.19: Vinyl cut out around window

5. Continue to apply the vinyl planks to all the exterior walls.
6. Next, add square end posts to the four corners of the house to cover the ends of the vinyl planks. The size of the corner posts in this example is 1.25, 17.7, 1.25 studs.
7. Now, replace your interior grayboxed props with the final assets. You can use the models we created in *Chapter 1* or the ones found in the **Prop Pack** listed in the *Technical requirements* section at the start of this chapter:

Figure 6.20: Final props placed

8. Next, insert a square part into the front entrance and rescale it to the dimensions of the doorway. This will be our front door. Insert a cylinder part and rotate it 90 degrees.

9. Rescale the cylinder part to 0.85, 0.25, 0.25 studs and place it on the door where you want your doorknob to be.

10. Now, rescale the cylinder part again so that the cylinder sticks through to the opposite side of the door by an equal amount. Insert a sphere part and scale it to 0.6, 0.6, 0.6 studs, and place it onto the cylinder part to create a doorknob.

11. Duplicate the sphere part and move it to the other side of the door:

Figure 6.21: Door handle

12. Select all the door parts and group them together.
13. Rename the model `Door`.
14. Select all the parts inside of the door model and turn their collisions off by disabling **CanCollide** so that people can walk through the door.
15. Duplicate the door and place it in all the house's doorways.

This completes the basic step-by-step process of creating a house in Roblox Studio out of primitive parts:

Figure 6.22: Completed house

With the conclusion of this chapter, we now have a completed house ready to move into. Through following the steps within this chapter, we have learned an efficient workflow for creating interior layouts for houses, as well as the steps to building it out. This, of course, is a skill that goes beyond building homes. It works for essentially any structure or even map that requires a sense of layout. With this newfound knowledge of creating layouts, we will move into *Chapter 7*, where we will be using these skills to design a single-player game map. See you then!

7
Single-Player Map Flow

In *Chapter 5*, we examined the steps to create a fluid multiplayer map. Now, we will examine the very different flow that follows in creating a single-player experience. In this chapter, we will examine the map flow that popular platform titles such as *Piggy* or *Doors* follow.

We will first look at how to plan the **first-time user experience** (**FTUE**), which will work like a non-intrusive tutorial that gives players a feel for the game. We will then plan out the layout for the map from start to finish so that we can create a linear path that leads to the finish. Next, we will create hints within the environment that will allow the player to continue moving forward without getting stuck or lost. Since progression is a key element in single-player experiences, we will see how to incorporate it into our game using a locked door and drawbridge whereby players must manually pull a lever to advance in the level. Finally, we will wrap up the level by adding ambient sound and lighting to the map.

In the following chapter, we will be looking at the following topics:

- Planning your map
- Drawing the player forward
- Creating a locked door
- Adding obstacles
- Building out the map
- Creating an atmosphere with lighting
- Adding ambient sounds

Technical requirements

You will need to open an empty baseplate in the latest version of Roblox Studio downloaded (at the time of writing, version 572). You will also need to insert the `Chapter 7` model pack, which can be found here: `roblox.com/library/14959208937`. Optionally, you can also have the **Light Editor** and **3Dtext Generator** plugins, which can be downloaded from `www.roblox.com/library/1223999426` and `www.roblox.com/library/2273628561` respectively.

All code used through this chapter can be found inside the `Chapter 7` folder at `https://packt.link/gbz/9781805121596`.

Planning your map

Before we begin building, we must first plan it out. Single-player maps are heavily story-driven, so as you think about your map, you should also be thinking about ways that you can hint at the story. For example, a level that takes place in a medieval castle illuminated only by old lanterns paints a clear picture of the time, place, and theme of the game. Another important aspect to consider when planning the first game level is the FTUE. Having a good FTUE ensures that the player remains engaged and does not get confused, resulting in them leaving the game. The FTUE usually runs the players through the first level and gives them an opportunity to get familiar with the different aspects of the game. With all of these points in mind, let's look at how we can do it.

How to do it...

We will begin by laying out the map in a 2D top-down perspective style using square parts. As we lay the map out, we will place door-size reference parts so that we can later build walls around them with consistent spacing for the door. We will then place the locked door and key, and then create a sinkhole in the tunnel for our obby to go. To finish, we will use the **3Dtext Generator** plugin to label the areas of the map accordingly. To begin, follow these steps:

1. Insert a square part and rescale it to the size of your spawn room. In this example, the part size is 75, 1, 50 studs. I suggest not making the spawn area too big as it may be harder to lead the players where they need to go.

2. Now, create a ledge using a square part that is 15 studs tall and 40 studs wide. Place it flush and center along the thinner side of the floor part. You should have 5-stud gaps on both sides of the ledge part that we just placed. Players will need to find a way to get on top of it in order to advance from the spawn area.

3. Next, create a hallway using a square part and attach it to the ledge part, as seen in *Figure 7.1*. The size of the hallway in this example is 25, 1, 75 studs long:

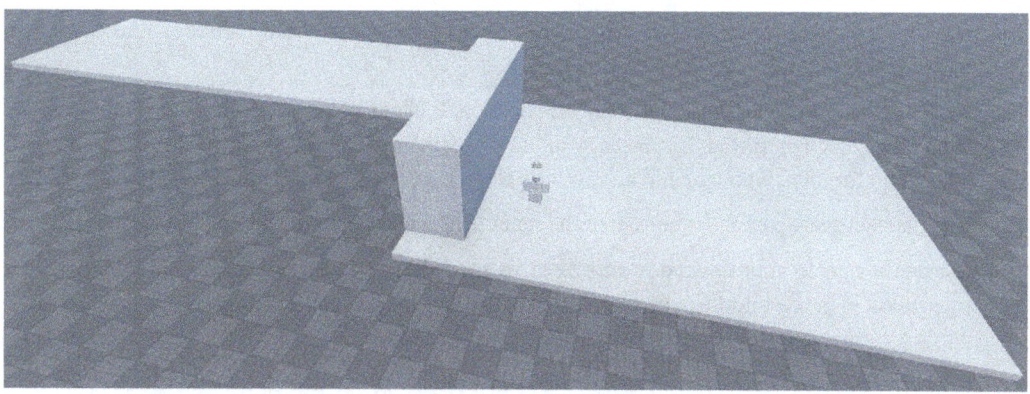

Figure 7.1: Starting area ledge

4. Create multiple rooms of varying sizes along the hallway that players will later explore to search for a key. In this example, I created four rooms connecting from the hallway.

5. Now, make a door part using a square part scaled to about `1, 10, 7` studs and place it at the entrance of one of the rooms.

6. Duplicate the door part and place the duplicates at the entrance of the remaining rooms.

7. Next, insert a square part and change its **Color** property to yellow (`255,255,0`).

8. Rescale the yellow part to be `17, 15, 1` studs.

9. Next, place the yellow-colored part at the end of the hallway to represent the locked door:

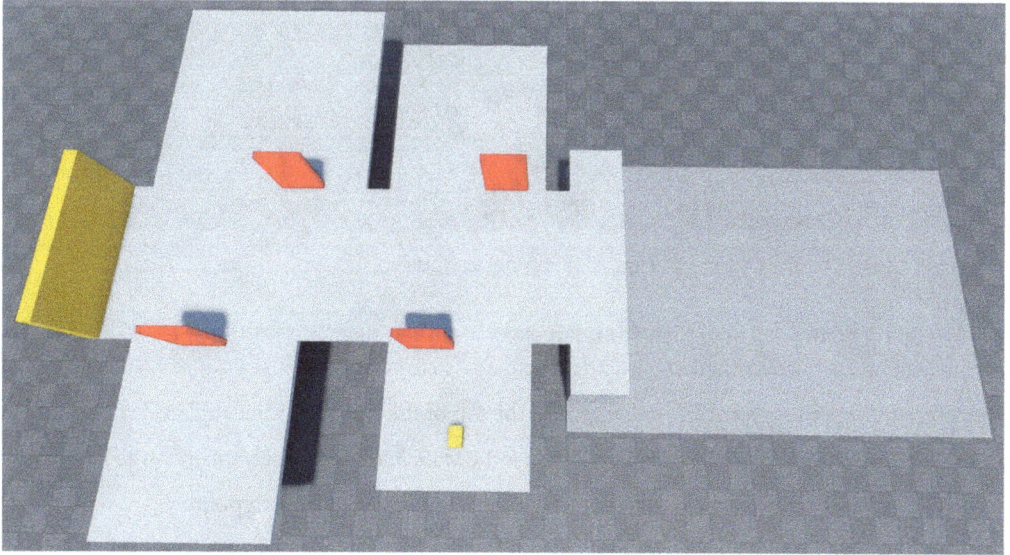

Figure 7.2: Hallway layout

10. Now, place a small, yellow-colored part inside one of the rooms on the floor to mark where we will place the key.

11. Create some stairs going down from the other side of the locked door. In this example, I created seven steps; each step was `0.75` studs tall and `1` stud wide. If your player has a hard time walking up the steps, you can add an invisible ramp part overtop of the stairs to add collisions.

12. Next, place a square part at the bottom of the stairs. This will become the floor of our metro tunnel.

13. Rescale the part to your desired room size. This room is going to be quite long and will have a large sinkhole in the middle, which will later create an obstacle course for players to overcome. In this example, the size of the room is `38, 1, 112` studs.

14. Now, create a hole in the middle of the part by duplicating the floor part, and then rescaling both of the floor parts so that a gap occurs where you want your hole to be. The hole in this example is `24` studs long. This will later become an obby that players must parkour through, so ensure that the hole is long enough.

15. Block off the sides of the sinkhole so that players can't get around. Since the theme of this example is based on an underground metro, I'm going to build some simple train tracks and a train beside the hole. This helps to work as a boundary, narrowing the width of the room and forcing the players to go a specific way:

Figure 7.3: Tunnel sinkhole

16. Create a `20`-stud-tall wall using a square part, and then move it past the hole all the way to the end of the train tunnel.

17. Attach a part to represent the hallway onto the top of the wall that we just placed.

18. Now, place a `20`-stud-tall truss object against the wall, leading the players up to the hallway.

19. Add a green color part at the end of the hallway to represent the finish point.

20. Next, use the **3Dtext Generator** plugin to label each of the rooms on your map. That concludes the steps of creating a thoughtful layout for your map.

You now have a full layout for your map, including blocker spots and where your future locked door and key will go:

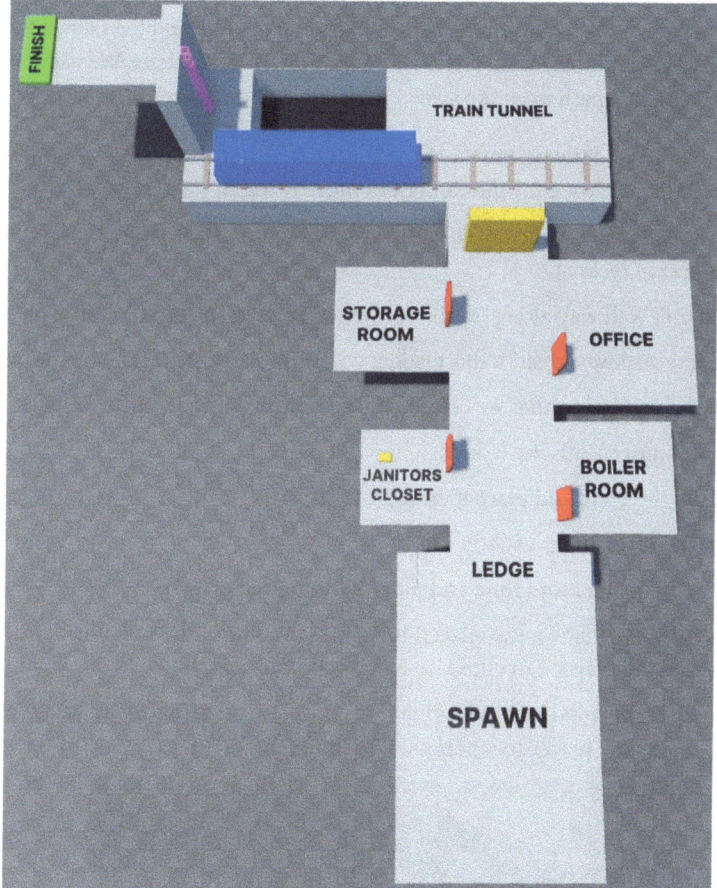

Figure 7.4: Completed layout

Having your map laid out before you begin building will make creating the rest of the map much more seamless and with less chance of having to adjust the size or layout after it's built.

Drawing the player forward

A well-designed story-driven map should drive the player linearly. This does not mean that the map must be a literal straight map; rather, it moves the player forward and does not have them getting confused as to where to go next. In this recipe, we will use a method that will help us achieve a proper forward map flow. The method that we will examine has a slightly out-of-reach ledge that the player must get up to advance in the level. This technique is simple, but simplicity is key if you want to avoid confusing players, especially at the starting level.

How to do it...

We will start by creating a ledge at the starting area, then create tall, vaulted walls around the perimeter. Next, we will create a path of planks extending from the ledge to the wall and then down the wall. We will then create a short ladder, and then stack crates at the bottom to create steps. We will finish this recipe by adding light fixtures and a path from the spawn to the start of the crates. To start, follow these steps:

1. Create tall walls around the perimeter of the starter area. In this example, the walls are 36 studs tall to allow adequate space for the camera to move around.

2. Next, build a thin plank walkway running along the top of the ledge that we laid out in the *Planning your map* recipe.

3. Extend the plank walkway along one of the walls, creating a jagged-looking path.

4. At the end of the walkway, create a short ladder going downward that is out of the reach of players.

5. Next, insert the crate prop that we created in the *Creating wooden crates* recipe of *Chapter 1*.

6. Place the crate underneath the ladder.

7. Now, duplicate the crate and place it on top of the first.

8. Scale down the crate on top slightly.

9. Duplicate the crate one more time and place it beside the first.

10. Scale down the crate that we just placed to be half the size of the one it is beside. This should create steps that the player can climb up to get onto the ladder.

11. Next, create a path of wood planks leading from the player spawn to the stacked wooden crates. This will help lead the player to where they need to go:

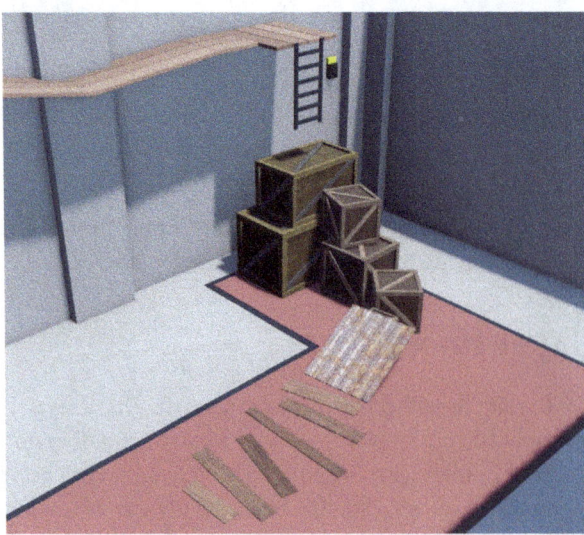

Figure 7.5: Stacked crates

12. Now, build or place the provided pallet model and then lean it against the box so that it looks like an accessible ramp.
13. Next, create some light fixtures that can attach to walls, such as an emergency light, torch, or lantern. Give them a pointlight to help illuminate the starting room.
14. Place the wall light fixtures that you created along the wall of the plank walkway. This will help light up the path that the player needs to follow.
15. Insert a **Spawn location** object and place it where you want players to spawn first.
16. Now, create a path of sorts leading from the player spawn location to the crates that we placed. In this example, I'm creating a dirt path, although stones, carpets, or even arrows can also be used. This is now a good time to play-test your game (*F5*) to make sure that it's not too challenging to climb up.

With that step completed, we now have the initial path from the spawn created:

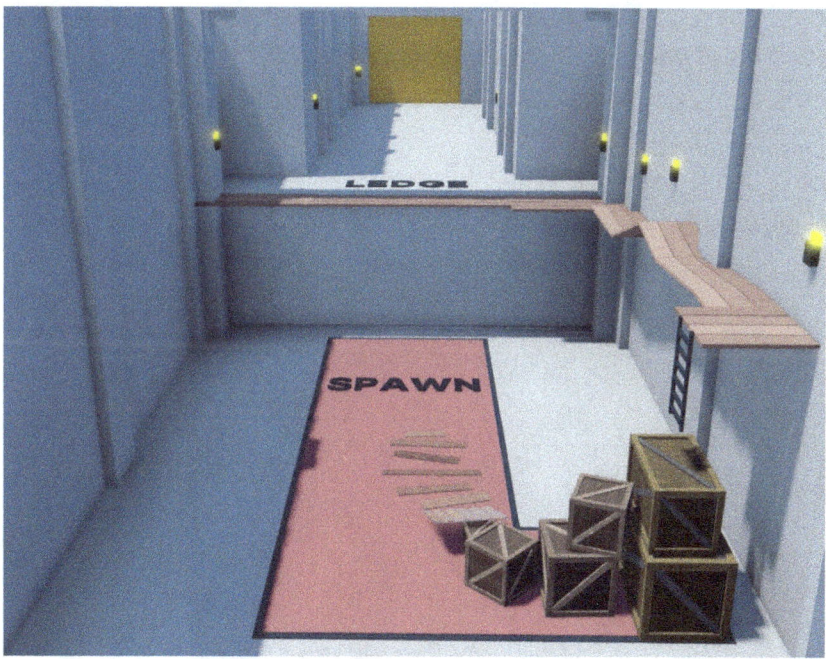

Figure 7.6: Completed path leading to the ledge

The players will instantly see the large open pathway over the top of the ledge but won't be able to jump up. They will quickly see the illuminated plank path leading from the ledge to the stack of crates that we created. Although we created an obvious path, the players will feel good as if they were the ones to figure out how to overcome the obstacle. Let's now look to see how to create our second challenge: locked doors.

Creating a locked door

As we learned in the *Drawing the player forward* recipe, having the player advance in a linear fashion is important for keeping the map flow. But if players are advancing too quickly, they will complete the levels too quickly and not be able to fully appreciate the map and atmosphere that you have created. To counter this, having locked doors can help spread out the time it takes to complete the level while still directing players forward. In this recipe, we will be now looking at how to utilize locked doors.

How to do it...

To start, we will insert the `Locked Door` model from the `Chapter 7` model pack and then ungroup it. We will then put the door in place and build walls around the hallway and rooms. Inside one of the rooms, we will build a shelf to place the key on, and then add a ceiling over the rooms and hallway. We will then finish by using a **SurfaceGui** object to create text above the doors. To begin, follow these steps:

1. Insert the **Locked Door** model from the `Chapter 7` folder.
2. Place the script inside of the model into the **ServerScriptService** object.
3. Next, ungroup the model.
4. Move the locked door to where you placed your yellow marker on the layout. It should fit inside of the wall, as seen in *Figure 7.7*:

Figure 7.7: Locked door

5. Now, move the corresponding key model to where you placed the key marker.

6. Delete the key and locked-door placeholder parts.
7. Now, with the door and key placed, build out the walls of the hallway around each room door.
8. Build some shelving at the back of one of the first hallway rooms, like what is seen in *Figure 7.8*.
9. Move the key model onto the shelf that we just built in the previous step:

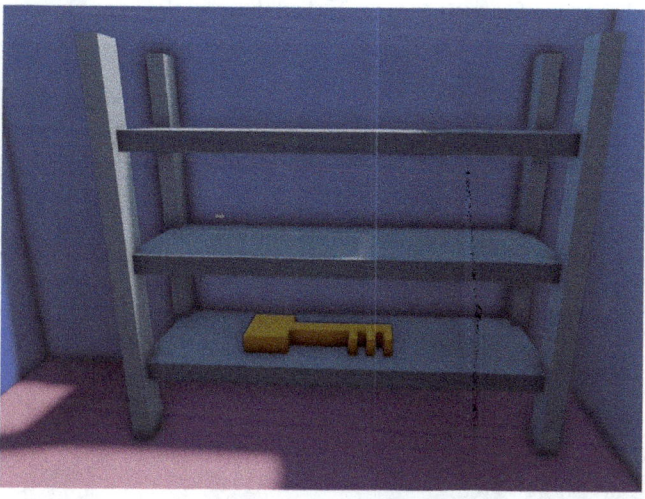

Figure 7.8: Key on shelf

10. Now, add baseboard to the bottom of the walls and ceiling board along the top of the hallway, as well as in each room attached to the hallway.
11. Next, place a `1.5`-stud-thick part across the top of the walls to create the walls' top board.
12. Place a part along the top of the walls to create a ceiling.
13. Build some frames around the doorways using thin square parts.
14. Next, add a square part above each of the doorways. We put text or the room number on this part to help the player differentiate locations from one another. To do so, insert a **SurfaceGui** object into the sign part.
15. Change the direction of the **Face** property of the **SurfaceGui** object so that it is showing on the front of the sign part.
16. Insert a **TextLabel** object into the **SurfaceGui** object.
17. Change the text inside of the **TextLabel** property box to say `ROOM 1`.
18. Now, change the **TextSize** property value. In this example, mine is set to `60`.
19. Change the **TextLabel** object's **BackgroundTransparency** property value to `1`.
20. Now, to center your text, change the **AnchorPoint** property value to `0.5, 0.5` and the **Position** value to `0.5, 0, 0.5, 0`.

21. Now, set the text's **Font** type. In this example, I will be keeping it to the default.

22. Change the **TextStrokeTransparency** property value to 0 to thicken the text.

Finally, add some light fixtures or torches along the walls of the hallway. Make sure each light fixture has a **Pointlight** object inserted. I also set the **Brightness** value of the pointlight to 0.75 to dim the light. That completes this recipe for setting up the locked door on the map:

Figure 7.9: Main hallway

You now know how to set up and use a very powerful tool: locked doors. This will help you pace your game so that players aren't able to continuously move forward. It also gives more purpose to the rooms and environment as players will need to explore and pay more attention in order to find the key. Let's now see how we can further create obstacles in the next recipe.

There's more...

Always make sure that your map has either a limited number of "fake" doors that can't be opened or that the doors that can be opened are very clearly indicated. Having too many doors, especially ones that all look the same, can be confusing to players.

Adding obstacles

Depending on your desired gameplay, obstacles can range from **non-player character** (**NPC**) guards to a puzzle minigame or even a simple parkour course that the player must pass. This helps amplify the gameplay and thus keeps the player engaged, encouraging them to stick around longer. In this recipe, we will use our previously learned knowledge of obstacle courses from *Chapter 5* to build out a simple parkour course that will lead players to the next area on the map.

How to do it...

To begin creating a parkour course that will lead players upward toward an illuminated ceiling, follow these steps:

1. Start by building walls along the train tunnel. The walls in this example are 31 studs tall.
2. Next, build out the walls around the finish point's hallway.
3. Add a 30-studs-tall and 56-studs-long part on top of the tunnel wall, starting at the back tunnel wall and stretching to roughly the start of the sinkhole, as seen in *Figure 7.10*:

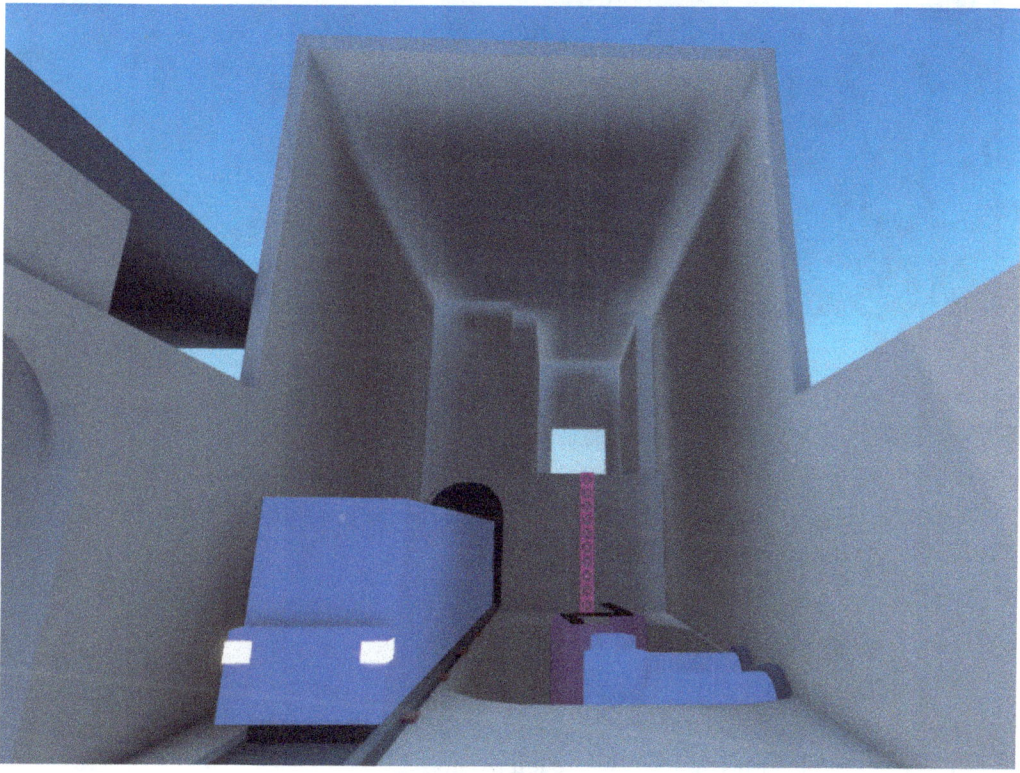

Figure 7.10: Vaulted ceiling

4. Using a square part, create a ceiling overtop of the walls that we just placed.
5. Now, create a hole in the ceiling, and then use square and wedge parts to make it look jagged, as seen in *Figure 7.11*:

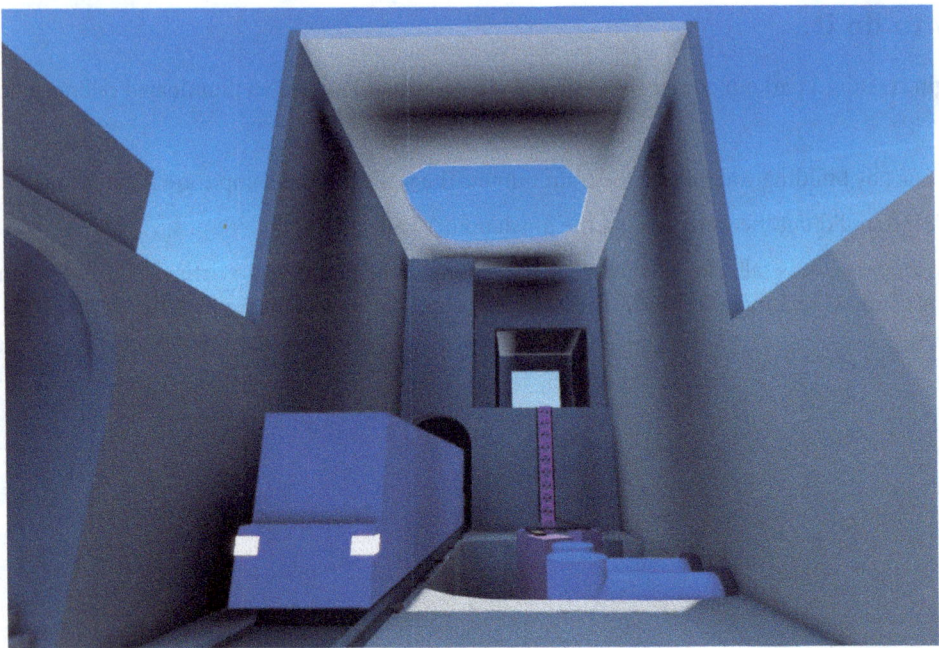

Figure 7.11: Hole created in the ceiling

6. Add a white neon part behind the hole at the top of the vaulted ceiling. This will catch players' attention from afar, drawing them toward where they need to go.

7. Now, add a large cylindrical part to the wall to create a pipe in a spot where players can see it as a platform to get across the hole in the floor.

8. Duplicate the part and rotate it 180 degrees.

9. Rescale the one end so that it's centered on the first pipe.

10. Now, add caps to the end of the pipe.

11. Next, create some pieces of debris, such as concrete pillars, extending upward from the sinkhole to create more platforms for the player to jump onto.

12. Duplicate the pillars of debris and then space them between 3 and 5 studs from each other so that players can jump from one to the next.

13. Now, place a thin plank connecting the debris and creating a path across some of the gaps in between the concrete pillars that we just placed.

You have created a direct and clear path, which was achieved with the brightly lit-up openings in both the ceiling and hallway. They act as clear indicators for which way the player needs to go to find the parkour course to get across the sinkhole. This simple yet engaging course adds a layer of challenge to help spice up your experience:

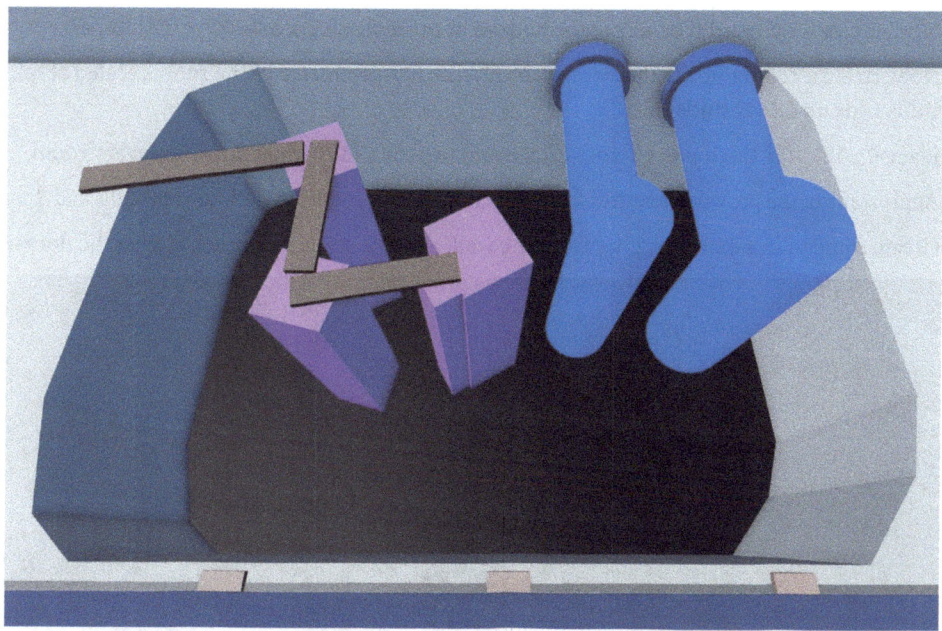

Figure 7.12: Obstacle course to get across the sinkhole

Building out the map

Now that we have the level designed and various blockers and obstacles along the way, we are ready to begin building out the map. As we do so, we will keep in mind what the story is that we're trying to convey to the player. If it is a horror map, perhaps you can build it out to look like a haunted mansion. Is it an old, abandoned mansion from the 1800s? If so, what kinds of props and items would you find decorating the different rooms? In this recipe's steps, we will be building out each room and area of our level to have its own unique theme, which is important for easy map navigation.

How to do it...

We will build out the remaining walls around the map and then add thin parts over the top of the walls to create different colored wallpaper in each room. After, we will decorate the walls by adding baseboard and ceiling board. We will build our windows and light fixtures and then finish by placing props around the map. To begin, follow these steps:

1. Start by building out any remaining walls needed on the map. There should be no gaps or missing walls that would allow players to escape.

2. Now, add a thin part 0.05 studs thick along the interior of the walls of each room. This will be the wallpaper, allowing us to give each room's walls a different color, the same as we did in *steps 8-10* of the *Building out the walls* recipe in *Chapter 6*.

3. Next, create baseboard trim along the bottom of the walls using a 0.25 x 3-stud part.
4. Now, create a ceiling board that wraps around the top perimeter of the rooms scaled about 3 studs wide and 1.5 studs thick.
5. Place 0.05-stud-thick parts across each room to create individual floors for every room.
6. Apply some of the provided textures from the Chapter 7 model pack onto your walls and floors.
7. Create some pillars extruding out from the wall, about 2 studs from each side of the doors:

Figure 7.13: Extruded doorway pillars

8. Add windows if applicable.

Use a dim-colored neon part with **Transparency** as 0 to light up the window and provide a sense of the time of day outside. For example, the window may be colored white to represent daytime or blue or black for night. This also limits how much of the out-of-bounds areas players can see, meaning we don't need to ensure that the outside is visually appealing if the player can't actually see out the window:

Figure 7.14: False window

9. Create ceilings by running a flat part across the top of the walls.
10. Now, create some shelving full of boxes and place the model along the wall of the hallway.
11. Next, create some wall-mounted light fixtures along the walls of the hallway.
12. Turn some of the **Neon** material on the light fixtures to the **Ice** material so that they look like they are burnt out. Place props in the spawn area. For example, place corroded barrels along the walls and scatter planks of wood across the floors, pipes running along the walls, and vents dangling from the ceiling. You can use arrows, bright colors, and neon lights to discreetly direct players toward their destination:

Figure 7.15: Discreet ways to draw the player forward

13. Next, place barrier props around areas that you don't want players to enter. These can include pylons, steel barricades, barbed wire, or even a glass panel.

14. Place props in each room, theming each room differently. In this example, I'm creating a boiler room, a janitor's closet, and two abandoned office spaces.

15. Lastly, create an obvious door using a white (244, 244, 244) neon part and place it at the end of the hallway where the finish is. With that, we have concluded this recipe.

You can see one of the finished scenes of the map in *Figure 7.16*, containing a nice balance of props without it seeming cluttered, as well as an appropriate use of neon and light to draw the player toward the needed destination:

Figure 7.16: Polished tunnel

We placed baseboard and ceiling board, something that we've done many times in previous chapters because it's a simple and familiar accent that adds great depth and shape to the walls, taking them from flat to defined. The placement of props throughout the map also helps make the map feel full and alive. So, with a now-polished and furnished map, let's see how we can further enhance it using volumetric lighting.

Creating an atmosphere with lighting

With our map now built out and filled with props, we can begin the process of adding volumetric lighting to the world space. We will use the provided Roblox lighting objects such as **SurfaceLight** and **PointLight** to illuminate the various regions of the map. We will use lanterns and fire to further create a sort of "flare" that will help lead players forward even in dark confined spaces.

How to do it...

We will create a light-emitting part using **SurfaceLight**, and then adjust the light object's properties. We will then duplicate it around the map to illuminate large rooms. We will then add pointlights to the wall-mounted light fixtures and fire and spotlights to the ceiling light fixtures. To start, follow these steps:

1. Create a large flat part positioned over the top of the starting room. It should be scaled roughly the width and length of the room.
2. Disable the parts' **CanCollide** property.
3. Next, insert a **SurfaceLight** object into the part.
4. If the light is being cast from the wrong direction, change the **EmissionFace** property.
5. Change the **Range** value to 45.
6. Change the surface light's color to fit the mood of the room. In this example, it's a dark orange (255, 176, 0), since I want the wall light fixtures to draw players toward the way to get on top of the ledge:

Figure 7.17: Janitor's closet with key

7. Next, insert a **PointLight** object into the wall-mounted light fixtures that we placed on the walls following the path up the ledge.
8. Next, duplicate the **SurfaceLight** part from *step 1* and move it to the long tunnel.
9. Rescale the part to the length of the tunnel, or according to where your light fixtures are.

10. Turn the light color's **Brightness** value to `0.75` since we don't want it to overpower the other light sources.

11. Now, insert a **SpotLight** object into the ceiling light fixtures.

12. Set the emission **Face** property of the spotlight. In this example, mine is set to **Bottom**. This sets the side of the part you desire the beam to be emitted from.

13. Change the **Angle** value to `180` degrees. The larger the number, the wider the region that the light will be cast.

14. Set the **Range** value that the light is casting evenly below. In this example, my **Range** value is set to `36`.

15. Change the **Color** value of the **SpotLight** object. In this example, the color is set to `166, 159, 133`.

16. Copy and paste the spotlight into the remaining light fixtures and adjust their individual ranges as necessary.

17. Place some static props that emit light, such as barrels that are on fire, candles, and flares.

That completes this recipe, meaning your map should be lit, metaphorically and literally:

Figure 7.18: Polished starting room

We will now go into the final recipe of the chapter.

There's more...

Finding the light source part can be a challenge, especially since they're usually invisible. A quick workaround is to use the **Light Editor** plugin by the Roblox developer *woo3*. This plugin marks where every light source is and its set color, making it easy to modify existing lighting on your map.

Adding ambient sounds

Fierce waves clashing against cliff walls, sharp fire crackles, and the whooshing of burst steam pipes. These are all sounds that make us feel specific feelings of fear, comfort, or perhaps curiosity. Sounds are a great way to encapsulate the mood of a particular room or object. In this final recipe, we will be completing our map by applying ambient sounds throughout our level. We will use the **Sound** object placed inside of a part and insert our own **SoundID** using the provided modifiable options found inside the property box.

How to do it...

We will create a cubed part, disable its collisions, and make it fully transparent. We will then insert a **Sound** object into it. Next, we will insert our desired audio ID and adjust its volume. Following this, we will insert a script into the part, which will allow the audio to automatically play. To finish, we will then place the sound parts around the map. To begin, follow these steps:

1. Start by inserting a square part into **Workspace**.
2. Rescale the part to be `1, 1, 1` studs.
3. Disable the **CanCollide** property.
4. Disable the **CanTouch** property.
5. Rename the part `AMBIENTSOUND_(insert sound name)`; for example, `AMBIENTSOUND_WindBlowing`, `AMBIENTSOUND_FireCrackling`, `AMBIENTSOUND_WaterDrops`, and `AMBIENTSOUND_StaticNoise`, which are used in this build.
6. Now, right-click the part inside **Workspace** and select **Insert Object**.
7. Select the **Sound** object.
8. Change the **SoundID** type to the sound that you would like to have play. For example, here are a few IDs that you can use:

    - Fire crackling: `236387093`
    - Water dripping: `9112902850`
    - Wind blowing: `9056932358`
    - Static: `6963538865`

9. Select the green **Play** icon found in the property box to play the sound clip and then adjust the **Volume** property accordingly.

10. Enable **Looped**. This will cause the audio to continuously repeat playing.

11. Change the **Range** value to however many studs away you want players to be able to hear the audio. In most cases, and in this example, the value is 36.

12. Insert the `SoundPlayer` script found inside the `Chapter 7` folder, or insert a script into the part and then type in the following code:

```
while true do
wait(0.1)
script.Parent.Sound:play()
end
```

13. Once you have created a range of ambient sound-emitting parts, begin placing them around the map in their set locations. Fire-crackling sounds can go into the barrels of fire, water-dripping sounds can be placed on the floor under pipes, and so on. That concludes the final step of this recipe.

You now know how to create and apply ambient sounds to your game.

Through this chapter, you have learned the key elements that make up an enjoyable single-player or story-based game; for example, how you thoughtfully planned the theme of your map and how you then reflected it in the map design and props used. You have utilized the use of an out-of-reach ledge to lead players forward and then challenged them to find a key for the door. You now have a solid foundation for your first level, which can easily be expanded on by continuing to use the knowledge that you've gained.

8
Building a PvP Map

What goes into designing and building the enjoyable player-versus-player maps that we see in popular games such as *Phantom Forces*, *Arsenal*, or *KAT*? One of the biggest considerations is how you can balance the map to give equal advantages for all of the players, while also encouraging players to strategize and work together in team-based game modes. In this chapter, we will be working on five key steps for successfully creating a balanced environment for such games – planning the **layout**, **grayboxing**, **prop placement**, **lighting**, and **polishing**.

As you follow along in this chapter, keep note of the common methods used for balancing the advantage points in various parts of the map, such as pathing and prop placement. Also, we will see how to incorporate risk and reward locations. By the end of this chapter, you will have a map ready for a wide variety of competitive gameplay.

In this chapter, we will be going over the following recipes:

- Planning your layout
- Grayboxing the map
- Risk-versus-reward spots
- Placing props for cover
- Creating an outer perimeter
- Adding volumetric lighting
- Finishing the map

Technical requirements

You will need the latest version of Roblox Studio downloaded (at the time of writing, version 572).

In this chapter, we will be building out of primitive parts, which can be found in the **Chapter 08 Building Kit** plugin located at `roblox.com/library/14959449724`.

All code used through this chapter can be found inside the `Chapter 8` folder at `https://packt.link/gbz/9781805121596`.

Alternatively, you can use parts directly from the **Part** drop-down menu found inside of Roblox Studio.

Planning your layout

The first step for creating maps, especially ones that require a balance between both sides of the map, is planning the layout. In this first recipe to kick off the chapter, we will be planning out how our map will look, the total size, and where our paths, objectives, and landmarks will be. We will then use labeled parts to build out a rough 2D version of the map. Remember – it's always quicker both short-term and long-term to properly plan and lay out your builds, as we have done throughout this book.

Getting ready

Open up Roblox Studio to an empty baseplate, and then insert the **Chapter 08 Building Kit** plugin found at `roblox.com/library/14959449724`.

How to do it…

To begin, we will scale a part to our map dimensions, then use wedge and corner wedge parts to create variety in the elevation along one side of the map. Next, we will build three paths that connect to the other side using a colored square part. Then, we will place colored parts on top representing buildings and non-enterable areas, and use the **ThreeDtext Generator** plugin to label each part. To start this recipe off, follow these steps:

1. Start by first inserting a square part into **Workspace** and then rescale it to be the baseplate that we will build this map upon. In this example, the part is `275, 2, 275` studs in dimensions. This will fit about 18-24 players comfortably.

   Map size will vary based on the gameplay style. Since Roblox is a socially driven platform, it's important that players don't feel alone in the map and that they do not have to walk for long distances to see other players. It's always good practice to see what the average map sizes are for popular games in the same genre that you're working on. This gives you an idea as to what the players may expect.

2. Next, place a `160, 11, 36`-stud square part along the back of one of the sides, starting from the corner of the baseplate. This will provide one of the initial teams of players with an elevated position. This also ensures that the map doesn't appear flat.

3. Duplicate the elevated part, then place the part along the original part, roughly in the center of the map. You can see this in *Figure 8.1*.

4. Using square parts, create stairs on both sides of the platform that we just placed. The stairs should lead down the baseplate, as seen in *Figure 8.1*:

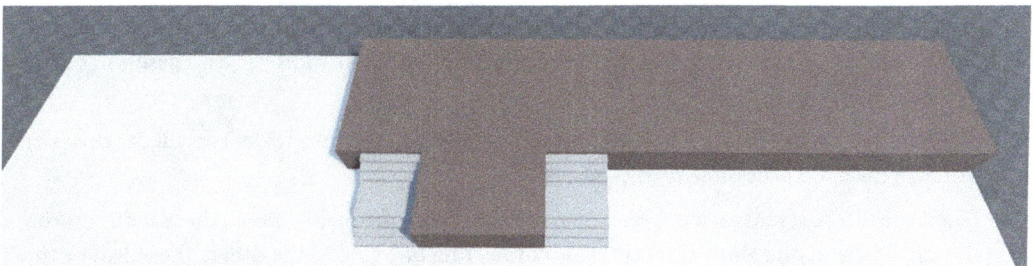

Figure 8.1: Elevated ground with stairs

5. Now, insert a wedge and corner wedge part provided in the **Chapter 08 Building Kit** or by using the **Parts** drop-down menu. Next, create slopes along both ends – I created an L-shape by running one of the wedges against one of the corner walls, visible in *Figure 8.2*.
6. Create a similar L-shaped slope along the opposite corner of the map.
7. Use a square part to build out a platform in between the stairs and in the corner of the L. This finishes the first team spawn area:

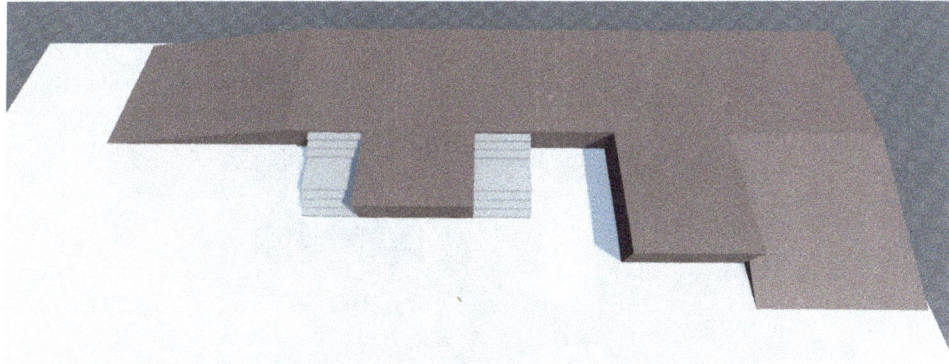

Figure 8.2: Elevated ground with stairs

8. Now, add a tall part, 1 stud thick, along the entire perimeter of the map to create a border wall.

   The wall should be about 4x taller than the players so that it's visually obvious that the wall represents out-of-bounds areas.
9. Now, insert a red-colored **SpawnLocation** object on top of the elevated side of the map.
10. Select the **SpawnLocation** object and change the **TeamColor** property to Bright Red (196, 40, 28), or a color of your choice.
11. Now, set the **Duration** value to 5. This is the amount of time in seconds that the player's force field will last when they spawn. The force field makes players invincible and helps reduce spawn killing.

12. Place a bright blue (13, 105, 172)-colored **SpawnLocation** object on the opposite end of the map from the red spawn and set its **TeamColor** and **Duration** values. These will be the two team spawn points.

13. Next, insert a square part and scale it flat and roughly 20-35 studs wide. We will use this part to create the main accessible paths.

14. Duplicate this part and create three separate paths down the map – one in the middle, one on the left side, and one along the right side connecting one side to the other. These will be the three main paths.

    It does not need to be a straight path – it can be windy, or have multiple corners – just remember that it should take roughly the same amount of time for players on each team to run to the same location on the map.

15. Fill in the remaining floor space with paths connecting all of these paths together. It should look something like what we can see in *Figure 8.3*:

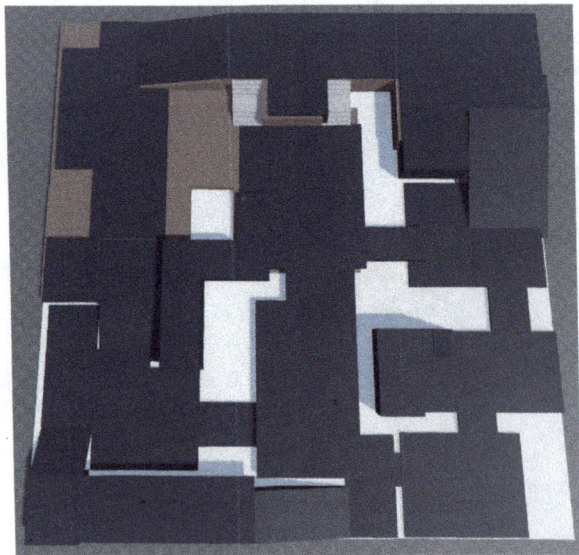

Figure 8.3: Paths around the map

16. Next, create a door and window part to use as scale references and place them around the map. Duplicate as necessary. We are placing these before placing our buildings because it is easier to build a flow-focused map this way.

    Every room should have at least two entrances on different sides of the building. Think of areas where players may camp. In *Figure 8.4*, you can see that since there are three entrances (indicated by the pink color), this makes it harder for players to sit in a corner and wait for someone to walk through the door. These doorways are purposely wider so that players have more room to move and peek around:

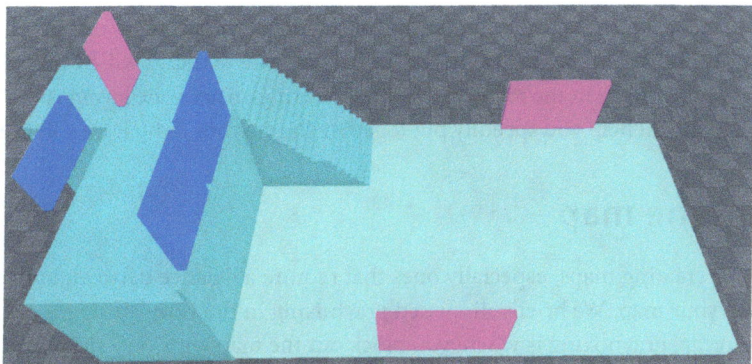

Figure 8.4: Interior layout example with door and window references

17. At every objective area, place a tall yellow part to represent where landmarks will go.

    Landmarks are usually tall enough to be visible across the map and operate as a beacon for players to use to navigate the map. In this example, I am building two watchtowers and a crane to indicate three points of the map that I want to draw players to.

18. Insert a flat square part anywhere you'd like to place a tunnel or archway, duplicating and resizing as necessary. In this example, I colored them `218, 0, 0`. Tunnels and archways provide variety, as well as a close-quartered environment that helps amp up players' excitement.

19. Now, open the **3Dtext Generator** plugin and create text on every colored part to label what it is, such as `Tunnel`, `Office Building`, `Watchtower`, `A site`, `B site`, and more.

This completes the first recipe; you should now have a laid-out map ready to graybox:

Figure 8.5: Finished layout

Notice how quick and easy it was to create a simple visual layout for an entire map. This will help speed up the entire development process, as you already know where things will be placed and where your paths lead. As you will see in the following recipes, creating an accurate layout is the foundation of building any map. It will help you speedily put together the graybox, which we will examine next.

Grayboxing the map

The second step for creating maps, especially ones that require a balance between both sides of the map, is to graybox your map. We briefly discussed grayboxing in the *Grayboxing the props* recipe of *Chapter 6*, but to recap, grayboxing is where you block out the map with very simplistic shapes and little to no detail.

In this recipe, we will be using primitive parts to graybox the walls and roofs around our previously created paths. After the initial main walls have been constructed, we will then go through and add extruding pillars on the walls, which will help create a less flat environment and provide the players with more cover.

How to do it...

In this recipe, we will block out the map along the paths that we created in the *Planning your layout* recipe using square parts. We will build walls around the enterable buildings and use door and window references to ensure they're accurately sized around the map. We will continue to block out the map by creating large door passageways. Lastly, we will go through the newly boxed-out buildings and add wedge parts to the roof and pillars extruding out from the walls around the map. To begin, follow these steps:

1. Insert a square part into **Workspace**.
2. Use the part to block out walls around the black paths we created in the *Planning your layout* recipe. The walls should be tall enough that players can't see over. The walls in this example average around 27 studs tall in most areas.
3. Build walls around the door and window reference parts that we placed in *step 15* of the *Planning your layout* recipe.
4. Delete the window and door reference parts. This should leave you with holes where the door and windows were:

Grayboxing the map 149

Figure 8.6: Walls built around where the reference parts were

5. Create a massive doorway on one of the main paths of the map. The doorway in this example is 30 studs wide.

6. Next, create two large doors – both ajar in opposite directions. This will help break up the line of sight so that players can travel down the middle of the map without being spotted as easily:

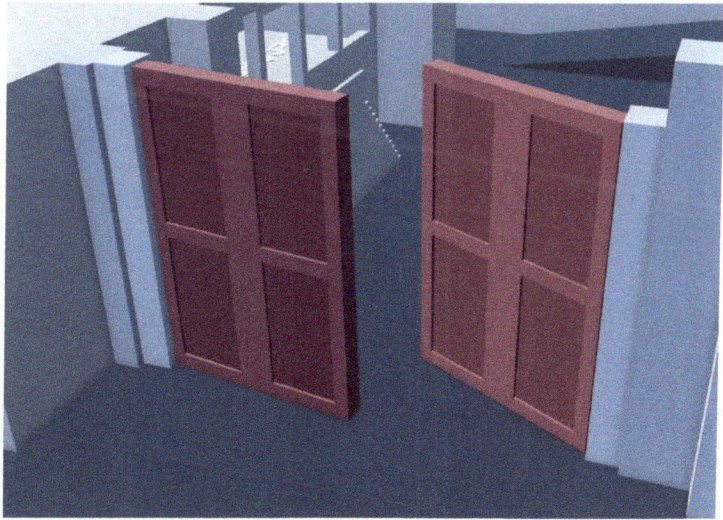

Figure 8.7: Doors slightly ajar

7. Block out your archways and tunnels by adding walls and a ceiling part matching the length of your placeholder part. You should have a boxy-looking tunnel or archway.

8. Now, add arch mesh parts provided in the **Chapter 08 folder Build Kit** and place them along the tops of the tunnels to round them:

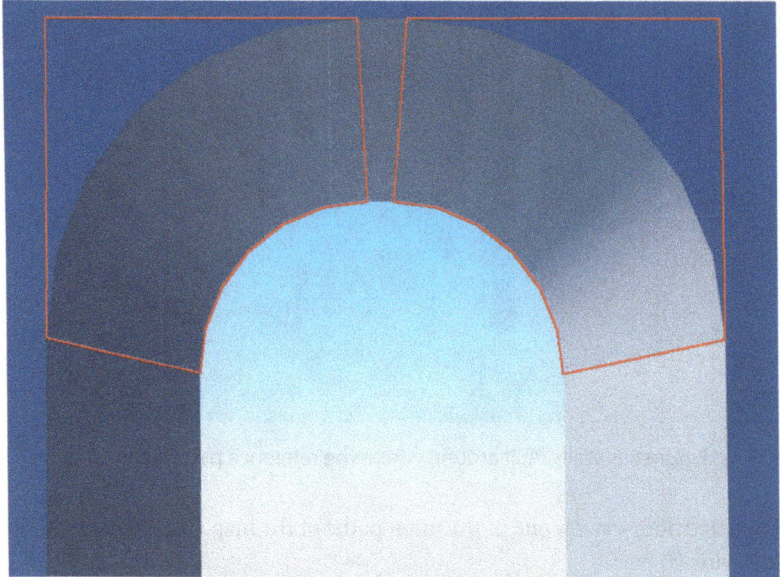

Figure 8.8: Archway parts placed on tunnel ceiling

9. Now, finish creating walls out of square parts along the remaining paths.
10. Next, add a `1`-stud-wide part along the center of the top of any building you wish to style with a sloped roof. This part will make it quicker for us to scale the wedges to an even side.
11. Rescale the center part to as tall as you want the roof pitch to be.
12. Add wedge parts on both sides of the center part to create a sloped roof:

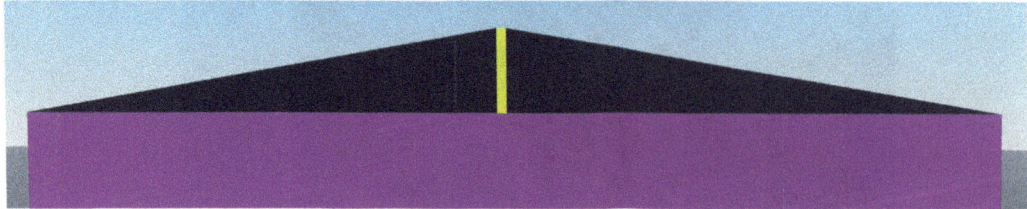

Figure 8.9: Sloped roof

13. Now, add some thick square pillars scaled about `5, 18, 5` studs large in any area on the map that is too large and open, such as in the middle of this open room in *Figure 8.10*. This will help provide cover over the open area:

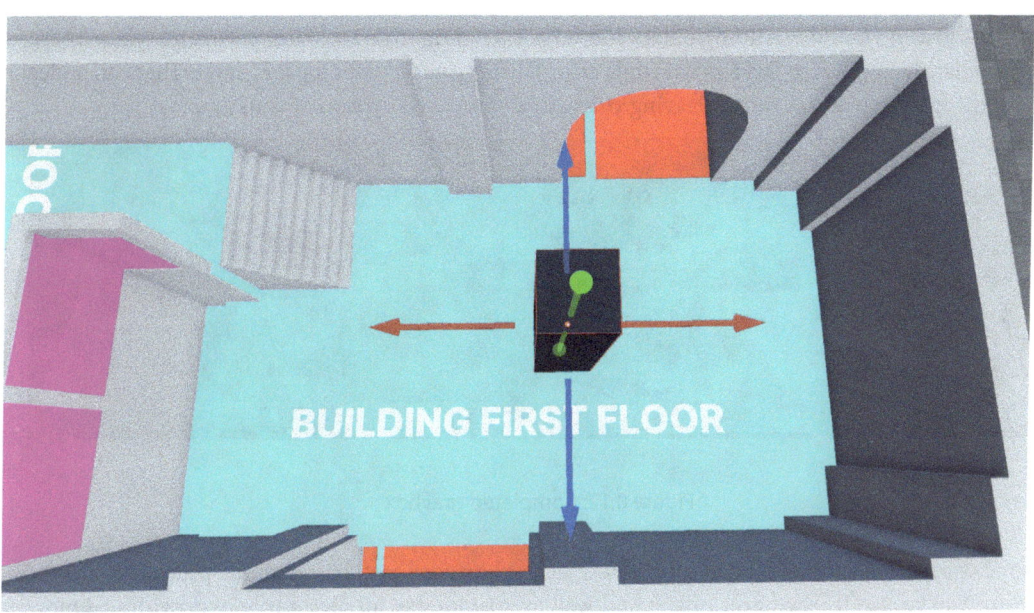

Figure 8.10: Pillar placed in an open area to provide cover

14. Add some 1-stud-thick and 3-stud-wide pillars on each side of the doors around the map. Move each pillar over about 2 studs from the edge of the doorway, as seen in *Figure 8.11*:

Figure 8.11: Door pillars

15. As in *step 13*, add extruding pillars and walls extruding from the outer perimeter walls. These pillars help the map feel less flat while also providing basic cover for the player. That concludes the final step of this recipe, leaving you with a grayboxed version of your map:

Figure 8.12: Completed graybox

You now have a deeper understanding of how to graybox your map based on the previously created layout. You've also learned how pillars and wall extrusions can all play a role in providing a more dynamic environment as well as helping balance out areas in the map. Let's now examine another way to introduce dynamic gameplay in the following recipe.

Risk-versus-reward spots

Every well-designed competitive game map that you play has what we call "risky spots." These are spots that are challenging to get to and usually provide little cover, but it's usually in a vantage point that allows you to see across the map. This means you have a better line of sight for spotting enemies. In this recipe, we will be going through our map and creating a watchtower that players can climb up on both sides of the map.

How to do it...

To begin, we will use square parts to block out the first watchtower. We will build its upper walls and roof, then attach a truss part to work as a climbable ladder. Next, we'll group and name the model, and then duplicate it over to the other side of the map. To start, follow these steps:

1. First, insert a square part into **Workspace** and scale it to the desired dimensions for the watchtower. In this example, the part is scaled `9, 33, 9` studs.
2. At the top of the watchtower, build a 2-stud-tall pony wall around the perimeter at the top of the tower to give the player inside some cover.
3. Select the four pony-wall parts and duplicate them.
4. Move the duplicated parts upward `15` studs.

5. Add another part 1 stud tall across the top of the four previously duplicated parts to create a ceiling.
6. Add four equally scaled corner wedges to each corner of the ceiling part to create a pointed roof. In this example, the corner wedges are `2.25 x 2.25` wide.
7. Now, add a `1x1`-stud pillar on all four corners of the pony wall and scale them to connect with the underside of the roof.
8. Insert a truss part and place it on one of the sides of the watchtower.
9. Rescale the truss part to the height of the watchtower.
10. Extrude the truss part halfway into the wall of the watchtower so that only half of the truss is visibly sticking out of the wall.
11. Select the individual part of the pony wall touching the truss.
12. Duplicate the pony-wall part.
13. Rescale both parts so that there's a gap to allow players to climb from the truss into the watchtower.
14. Select all the parts of the watchtower.
15. Group and rename the model `Watchtower_01`.
16. Duplicate the watchtower and move it to the opposite side of the map. That concludes the final step of this recipe, leaving you with two areas that offer high risk with an equally high reward:

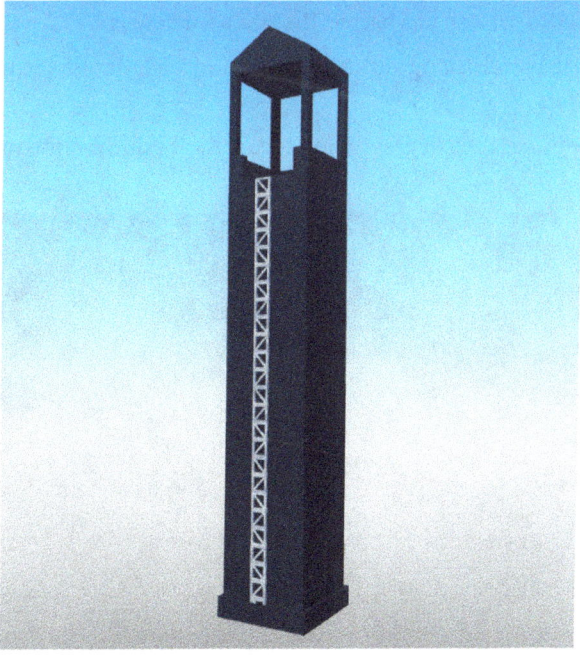

Figure 8.13: Completed watchtower

You now understand how you can use resourceful locations that players have to take a risk to get to, creating more aggressive gameplay approaches that players can take. This not only helps spice up the gameplay but also adds a fun "king of the kill"-type competition among players. Now, let's dive into the next recipe to see how we can balance out the map while also creating an immersive environment.

Placing props for cover

Now that we have created the shell of our map, we are ready to go through and begin placing parts to represent the graybox of where the props will go. We will place the props in areas that will provide adequate cover, while also not being too much of an advantage. Some of the props that we will be adding are for the aesthetic of the game, which will help encapsulate the theme of the map.

How to do it...

First, we will start at one end of the map and begin placing cylinder parts that will represent barrels and stacks of tires. We will then build out the shape and size of crates, a car, and a fountain, and place them accordingly. We will ensure that every area is completely balanced with how much cover is provided. To begin this recipe, follow these steps:

1. Insert a cylinder part into **Workspace** and change its color. You will use this color throughout this recipe to represent props. In this example, I'm using 45, 100, 245.

2. Rescale the cylinder to the size of a barrel. The size used here is 5.35, 3.9, 3.75 studs.

3. Duplicate and place barrels along various corners and walls across the map to help provide protection for players.

4. Rotate one of the barrels 90 degrees and place it flat beside a crate to create a spot with defensive cover:

Figure 8.14: Graybox props providing cover

5. Next, insert a square part onto the ground path.
6. Rescale the part to the size of a shipping container, about `10, 10, 18` studs.
7. Place the shipping container box in a couple of spots around the map.
8. Create a stack of barrels beside one of the shipping containers so that players can climb up on top.
9. Now, insert another square part about `5, 5, 5` studs to create a crate.
10. Duplicate the crate model and place it across the map.
11. Rescale some of the crates so that they differ in size.
12. Block out the shape of a car along one of the outer perimeter walls.
13. Create a few climbable stacks of crates along inner walls and platforms so that players can jump up and get to different areas quicker.
14. Add an `8, 2, 8`-stud cylinder part beside the non-elevated team spawn area toward the middle of the map. This will be a fountain.
15. Duplicate the cylinder part on top of itself and create a centerpiece. This concludes the steps for grayboxing props into your map. Your map should now be filled with grayboxed props to be placed around the map:

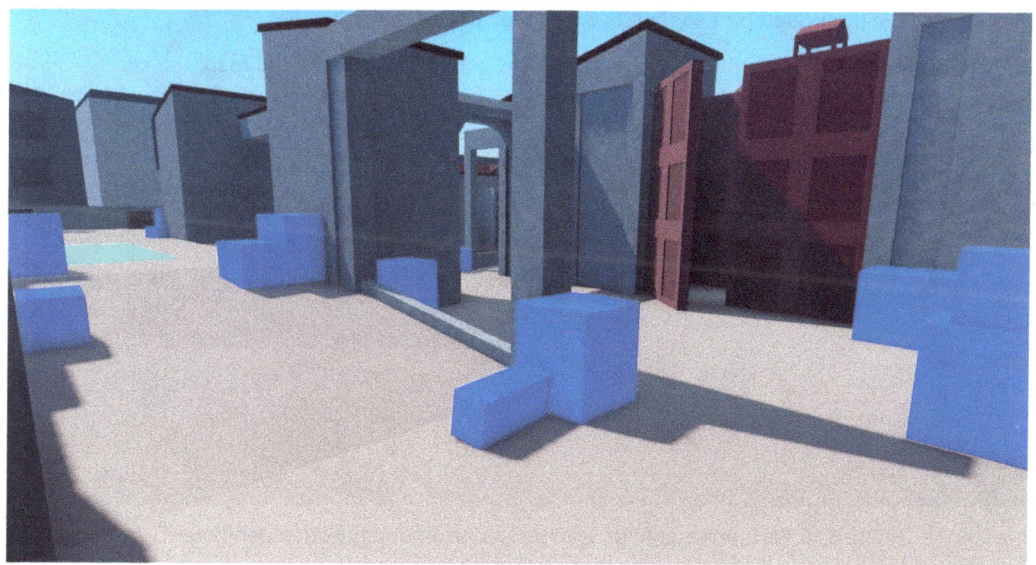

Figure 8.15: Map filled with grayboxed props

Completing this step now provides you with the tools and knowledge to place props with appropriate spacing to avoid causing clutter. You also now have consistent cover for players to hide behind or scale to get to higher vantage areas. Now, let's see how we can further expand on the map in the following recipe.

Creating an outer perimeter

With our main map's graybox now complete, we will now create buildings and objects to tower over and surround the four edges of the map. This will help affirm with players where the boundaries are. After we roughly block out the buildings, we will then do a quick pass on up-ressing (increasing detail) the buildings by adding wedges to create a roof, chimneys, windows, and false doors.

How to do it…

To start this recipe, we will be using square parts to block out the general shape and size of the buildings that we will place around the outer perimeter of the map. After placing the building walls, we will then use wedge parts to create roofs. Finally, we will go through each of the blocked buildings and carve out holes for where the doors and windows will go. To begin, follow these steps:

1. Insert a square part into **Workspace** and scale it to `35, 28, 30` studs.
2. Place the part along one of the walls on the outer perimeter. This will be the outer shell of a building.
3. Duplicate the building part and move it over beside the original.
4. Rescale the duplicated part so that it's a different size from the last.
5. Continue to place the building parts around the entire perimeter of the map:

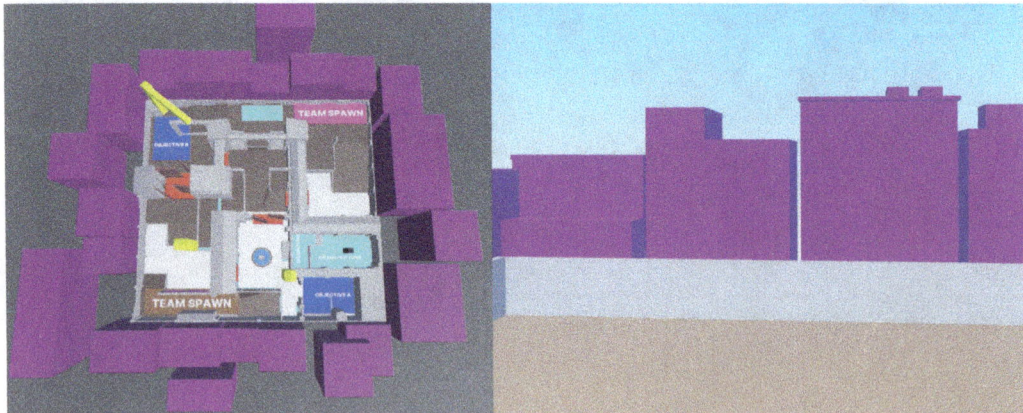

Figure 8.16: Parts representing buildings placed around the outer perimeter

6. Add center parts along the top center of each of the building parts that you want to have a sloped roof, like what we did in *steps 10* and *11* of the *Grayboxing the map* recipe.
7. Add wedge parts to both sides of the center tops to create sloped roofs.
8. On any flat-topped buildings, build a short pony wall around the top perimeter.

9. Move each of the four pony walls inward 0.25 studs so that it leaves a small gap, giving the building more depth.
10. Place a flat part on the rooftop and give it a different color. The flat-topped roofs should look like what's shown in *Figure 8.17*:

Figure 8.17: Pony wall around rooftop

11. Next, insert a square part to use as a window reference. Size accordingly and duplicate as necessary.
12. Place the window parts along the front of all the outer buildings.
13. Create an overhang using a wedge part on some of the windows.
14. Now, create some extruding parts around the wall to give more depth to the buildings. With that complete, this concludes the final step of this recipe, leaving you with some simply blocked-out buildings to help create boundaries on the map:

Figure 8.18: Finished grayboxed perimeter buildings

You now know how to optimally create background buildings for your maps. These provide not only a sense of boundary but also help make the environment feel real and not like a floating baseplate. Let's now dive into the next recipe to see how we can turn the map alive using volumetric lighting.

Adding volumetric lighting

In this recipe, we will be looking at the best methods when applying and modifying volumetric and global lighting in Roblox. First, we will be working with surface lights to illuminate the interior of buildings. Next, we will graybox some streetlamps and light fixtures to which we will then add PointLights, giving us a more suitable range of effects that we can't get with a surface light. We will finish off this recipe by modifying the global lighting properties to give the environment its desired ambiance.

How to do it...

To begin, we will insert a flat square part and turn its collisions off as well as make it fully transparent. We will then insert a **SurfaceLight** object into the part and begin placing and duplicating the light part inside buildings and tunnels. We will then create some simple light fixtures using square and cylinder parts, and then attach a **PointLight** object to illuminate the fixture. Lastly, we will add **ColorCorrection** and **SunRay** objects to the global lighting and modify their properties to fit our desired style. Let's see how we can accomplish this in the following steps:

1. Start by inserting a square part into **Workspace**.
2. Rescale the part to be `0.25` studs tall on the *y* axis.
3. Change the part's color to `255, 255, 0`.
4. Change the part's name to `SurfaceLightPart`.
5. Right-click the part and insert a surface light.
6. Change the part's **Transparency** value to `1`.
7. Select the part and move it to the top inside of a dark zone in the map, such as a tunnel or building interior.
8. Select the surface light and then modify the number in the **Range** box so that it properly illuminates the area. In this example, the range is set to `42`.
9. Modify the surface light's **Angle** property to adjust the angle at which the light is being emitted. In this example, the angle is set to `185` degrees.
10. Duplicate the surface light part and place it in every large room and area that needs brightening up, as seen in *Figure 8.19*. Alternatively, you can use **Pointlight** or **Spotlight** objects to illuminate the interiors of buildings. Play around to see what feels right for your use case.
11. In the **Lighting** object inside of the Explorer, change the **Ambient** value to `42, 42, 42`.
12. Now, build a simple block-out of a streetlamp post if you didn't create one while grayboxing the props. Make sure it has a part or attachment that we can attach a spotlight to.
13. Insert a **SpotLight** object into the streetlamp.
14. Change the spotlight's **Face** property so that it is emitting from the correct direction.

15. Modify the **Range** value of the spotlight so that it illuminates everything below it. In this example, my range is set to 45:

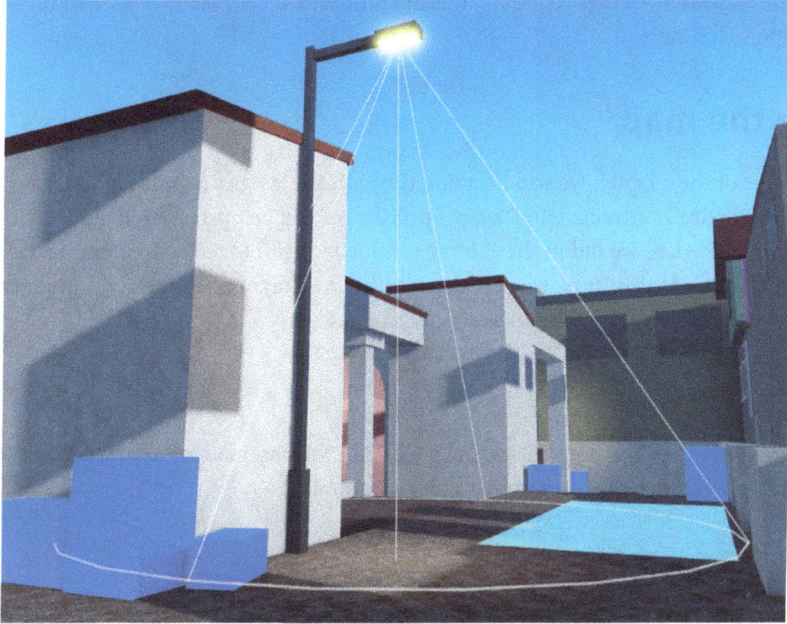

Figure 8.19: Street lamp with an attached spotlight

16. Change the **Angle** value. In this example, it is set to 69 degrees.
17. Group and then rename the streetlamp model `StreetLamp`.
18. Duplicate the streetlamp to other areas of the map. This concludes the final step of this recipe. You can see a comparison and how much of an impact adding some basic surface lights will have for brightening up your map interiors:

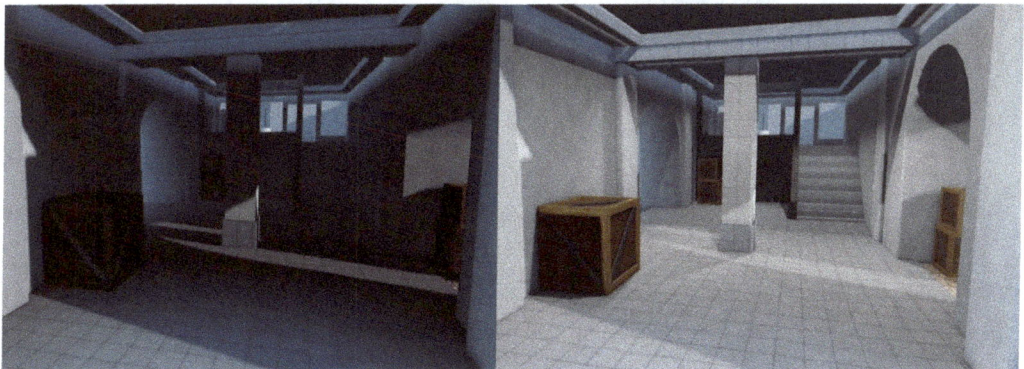

Figure 8.20: Interior with and without a surface light applied

You now have a solid understanding of the different use cases for both surface lights and spot lights. You've successfully illuminated the dark shadowy areas of your map and tied the whole scene together by modifying the various attributes to global lighting properties. Let's see how we can finish the map in the final recipe to follow.

Finishing the map

For the final recipe of the chapter, we will be going through the last process needed to finish building a successful and stylistically attractive PvP map – polish. We will be up-ressing the quality of the map from graybox to polished, as we did in the *Adding volumetric lighting* recipe to increase the fidelity of the buildings and walls. At this time, we will also replace the grayboxed props with their final assets and finish off by coloring and applying materials across the map.

Getting ready

You will need to insert the `Chapter 8` model pack onto the baseplate or use assets that we created previously in *Chapter 1*, such as crates, cacti, tables, and desks.

How to do it...

To begin, we will be using primitive-shaped parts to layer on ledge details and extrusions to buildings and main walls around the map. We will then go inside and add baseboard and ceiling board to the building interiors. Next, we'll replace the grayboxed props with the final assets provided in the `Chapter 8` model pack, or any existing assets that you have available. Lastly, we will apply color and material to the map. To begin, follow these steps:

1. Add 1-stud-thick parts that overhang the rooftops of each building by about 3 studs:

Figure 8.21: Overhanging roof

2. Next, add ledges roughly in the middle of the building wrapping around the wall.

3. Now, add a baseboard along the bottom of the interior walls of each enterable building on the map. The baseboard size in this example is 0.25 studs tall and 0.15 studs thick.
4. As in *step 3*, add a ceiling board around the top perimeter of each ceiling. The ceiling board size in this recipe is 2 studs thick and 1 stud tall.
5. Now, go through the map and replace each of the grayboxed props with their final assets.
6. Add a 0.15-stud-thick and 2-stud-tall part along the exterior base of each building wall.
7. Add a square cap along the top of each perimeter wall.
8. Recolor your map.
9. Next, add materials to your map if you don't wish for it to remain looking like plastic.
10. Next, right-click on the **Lighting** property and insert **SunRayEffect** shader effects.
11. Adjust the **Intensity** value of the sun rays to 0.23.
12. Now, right-click on the **Lighting** property again and insert **ColorCorrection** shader effects.
13. Modify the **Saturation** property to 0.3.
14. Modify the **Contrast** property box numbers within the **ColorCorrection** shader to 0.15. This concludes the final step of the recipe and chapter. You now have a completed map ready for action:

Figure 8.22: Completed PvP map

Congratulations! You've created a high-quality map that you can use for a variety of gameplay options. You have learned how to efficiently plan and lay out a balanced, well-pathed map. You used your skills of working with primitive parts to create a graybox, which you then refined into a polished state.

You now understand the importance of prop placement and how their positioning and scale can throw off the entire balance of the map. As you go forward in this book, remember that the steps to building anything are essentially the same, whether it be a prop, a house, or an entire map. Remember – plan the layout, graybox, prop placement, lighting, and polishing. Let's see what the next chapter has in store.

9
Monetizing Your Experience

By following the various recipes provided in this cookbook, you've learned how to build a wide variety of gameplay experiences. Now you are experienced and almost prepared to earn some Robux. This chapter will examine several ways that you can do so using built-in Roblox features such as **gamepasses** and **Developer Products**. We will also examine use cases for **paid access** and subscription-based **private servers**. Lastly, we will look at how we can retain premium players in our game by offering exclusive items behind a premium-member-only door, allowing us to generate passive-engagement-based income.

In this chapter, we will be looking at the five main ways to help monetize your experiences:

- Gamepasses
- Developer products
- Paid access
- Private servers
- Engagement-based payouts

Technical requirements

For this chapter, you will need to open your experience with the latest version of Roblox Studio as well as the game's configuration page found in **Creator Dashboard**.

You will also need to download the provided assets and scripts, including the tip jar model, icon template, and `PremiumDoorScript`, which are all provided here: https://packt.link/gbz/9781805121596.

Gamepasses

Gamepasses are a great and simple way to monetize your experience through a one-time fee. Once a pass has been purchased, it often rewards the user with some sort of in-game perk or item. In this recipe, we will examine how to create a gamepass that rewards the player with gear of our choosing.

How to do it...

We will begin this recipe by creating an icon using the provided template. Next, we will create a new gamepass and set the image, title, and description. After uploading the gamepass, we will put it up for sale and change the price. We will then open Studio, insert a script into the **ServerScriptService** object, and place our gear of choice into the **ServerStorage** object. Finally, we will copy and paste the gamepass's **AssetID** object into the script. Let's see how:

1. To begin, you will need to create a 512x512 image for your gamepass icon. To do this, download the template provided in the Chapter 9 folder:

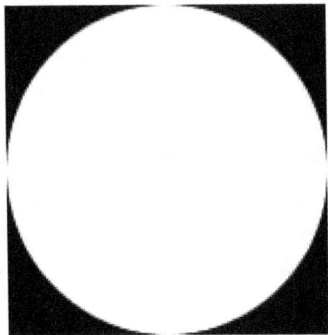

Figure 9.1: Icon template

Alternatively, if you do not upload an icon with the pass, Roblox will upload a default image that can be changed again later.

2. With the template downloaded, open it in your preferred image editing software such as Adobe Photoshop. A great free-to-use program for this can be downloaded at https://www.getpaint.net/download.html.

3. Create your icon design within the bounds of the circle. Anything outside of it will be cut off when you upload the image.

4. Next, save the image as a .jpg, .png, or .bmp file.

5. Now, open **Creator Dashboard** on the Roblox website via the **Create** button at the top of the website.

6. Open the **Overview** page of the experience you would like to create a pass for by clicking on the experience's icon.

7. Navigate to the **Associated Items** tab under the **Content** section of the box located on the left-hand side of the screen.

8. Select **PASSES**.

9. Click **CREATE A PASS**.
10. Click **CHANGE** to open your file explorer.
11. Select an image you would like to use for the icon.
12. Rename your gamepass in the title box. The title should be kept short but highlight what the user is getting from purchasing the pass. For example, a pass that rewards double coins could be titled **2X COINS!**.
13. Fill in the description box with a brief paragraph or sentence explaining what purchasing the gamepass will give the player, or how it will benefit them. The more intensive your description, the higher likelihood someone will see the value in purchasing the item.
14. Click **CREATE PASS** at the bottom of the screen.
15. Now, we need to set the price of the gamepass. To do so, navigate back to the **Associated Items** tab in the experience overview and select **PASSES** again.
16. Select the pass that you just created to open its **Basic Settings** page.
17. Select **Sales** in the navigation bar on the left-hand side of the screen.
18. Next, toggle the **Item for Sale** option on.
19. Set the price of your pass in Robux.

    Since gamepasses are only a one-time purchase, they're usually set at a higher price compared to things such as Developer Products. But with that in mind, also remember that if it's too expensive, no one will buy it.

20. Navigate back to the **Associated Items** page.
21. Hover over the newly created gamepass and then select the three little dots that appear in the upper-right corner.
22. Select **Copy AssetID**. This copies the ID of the gamepass that we created, which we will use in a later step.

    Alternatively, you can find the ID by navigating to the **Assets** page on the website and then copying the number digits found in the webpage URL.

23. Now that the gamepass has been created, open the experience in Roblox Studio.
24. Insert the **GamepassItemGiver** script into the **ServerScriptService** object located inside the `Chapter 9` folder.
25. Next, insert a tool or gear that you would like to give the player into the **ServerStorage** object – for example, a speed coil, gravity coil, laser gun, and so on. Speed and gravity coils allow the player to move faster/jump higher by set increments. A laser gun is a common premium weapon.
26. Double-click the **GamepassItemGiver** script to open the script editor.

27. Beside the line where it says **gamepassId**, paste the **AssetID** value of the gamepass that we copied previously in *step 22*.

28. Now, copy the name of the tool that we inserted in *step 25*. In this example, the name I am inserting in between the quotation marks is `"Speed Coil"`. If you are giving more than one item, you can continue the same format as follows: `{"FlashLight", "Speed Coil", "GlowStick"}`. Make sure the script name matches the tool name.

That completes the first recipe of this chapter.

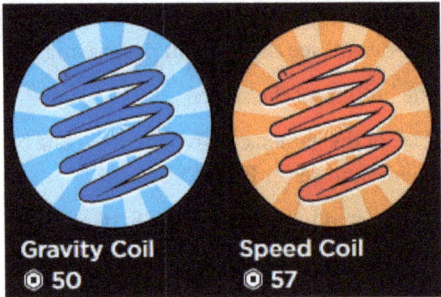

Figure 9.2: Gamepasses for sale

You now know how to create and upload your gamepass, as well as how to set it up to reward players with items who purchase the gamepass.

Developer products

Unlike gamepasses, developer products can be purchased multiple times. This works well for use cases such as purchasing in-game currency or limited-use perks. In this recipe, we will be setting up a donation tip jar that allows players to interact and purchase the "tip" through the use of developer products.

How to do it...

We will create a logo that we will then upload to a developer product. Next, we will update the **Title** and **Description** values and then set a **Price** value. We will then insert the tip jar model from the `Chapter 9` folder, and insert the correct developer product **AssetID** value into the script. To start, follow these steps:

1. To create an icon for our developer product, follow *steps 1-4* of the *Gamepasses* recipe. It follows the same `512x512` size and file format as the gamepass.
2. Navigate to **Creator Dashboard**.
3. Select an experience that you would like to create an item for.
4. Choose the **Associated Items** navigator tab found in the left-hand menu on the screen.
5. Now, select the **DEVELOPER PRODUCT** option.

6. Open the **Configure** page by selecting the **CREATE A DEVELOPER PRODUCT** button.
7. Upload your logo image.
8. Name your developer product. In this example, I am going to name it `TIP: 10 Robux`. Keep the title short and to the point.
9. Fill out a brief description of what the product is, does, or gives you. In this example, I am mentioning that this is a donation and will not reward the player with anything (besides good karma for tipping the devs, of course).
10. Set the price in Robux that you want to sell the item for.

    Since developer products can be purchased an unlimited number of times, you should think about setting the prices at affordable prices that entice players to buy again and again. If you have multiple dev products set up, you can get special deals and prices for more expensive items so that the player has both an affordable option and some other more tempting offers to consider.

11. Click the **CREATE DEVELOPER PRODUCT** button at the bottom of the page to publish the item.
12. Next, open your experience through Roblox Studio.
13. Insert the **Tip Jar** model from the `Chapter 9` folder.
14. Open the Model's dropdown and then double-click the script to open it.
15. Briefly minimize Roblox Studio, then navigate to the **Associated Items** tab of the experience's **Configure** page.
16. Copy the **AssetID** value of the dev product.
17. Back in Roblox Studio, paste the **AssetID** value in between quotation marks on the first line of the script.
18. Place the tip jar by the spawn in a highly visible location where players will see it.

Congratulations! You now have a working tip jar using a developer product that you created from scratch:

Figure 9.3: Finished tip jar

Developer products are easily one of the best ways to make passive income in your experience, and this is just one of the many ways that you can use them.

Paid access

On Roblox, a large number of games are released in their early alpha or beta stages as a paid-access experience. This is good for two main reasons. First, you're able to generate passive revenue to further fund the development of the project. Secondly, it allows us to filter how many people are entering the experience, which allows us to easily monitor the state of the game and feedback from the players. If something critical comes up, or you realize players don't enjoy certain things, it's easy to fix it now before you go through with an official game launch, which may end in bad user experiences and players not returning. Through this recipe, we will look at the steps for setting up paid access as well as some tips for pricing it.

How to do it...

We will start by opening Roblox Studio and navigating to the **Game Settings** menu where we will then set the game to **Public** and then enable paid access, setting our desired price. To begin, follow these steps:

1. To begin, navigate to the **Creator Dashboard** on Roblox.
2. Open your experience in Roblox Studio.
3. In the top bar of Studio, find the gear icon titled **Game Settings** found under the **Home** tab. This will open a pop-up menu for the game settings.
4. In the **Permissions** tab, make sure that the game is set to **Public** as you're unable to set paid access for a private experience.
5. Next, select the **Monetization** tab.
6. Scroll to the bottom of the popup and enable the **Paid Access Price** toggle.
7. Enter the price in Robux that you would like the charge the user.

   Note that this is a one-time purchase. Even if you change the price in the future, players who have purchased it will always retain access unless the game is set back to **Private**.
8. Select the **Save** button at the bottom of the popup.

Although this was a brief recipe, you now know why you may want to leverage the use of paid access for the early demo stages. Along with knowing the "why," you also know the "how" of enabling paid access for your experience.

There's more...

Paid access is a great way to get income while also being able to receive player feedback. When people invest time (or in this case, Robux) in your game, they are more likely to return. Because of this, even if the game has some issues with early access, players are still likely to keep coming back to see whether the issues have been fixed.

Private servers

Private servers work on a month-to-month subscription basis, allowing players to create their own private dedicated server that they can set up with their own parameters, such as who can join. Private servers can be made free, but many games have also seen success in monetizing off of the monthly charge. This is especially true with games that offer more in-depth customization or added perks within the experience exclusive to private servers. In this recipe, we will be examining how to enable and set prices on private servers.

How to do it...

We will start by opening the experience and enabling **Private** servers. We will then set our desired price and save our place settings. To begin, follow these steps:

1. Open up Roblox Studio to your desired experience.
2. Next, find and select the **Game Settings** icon within the **Home** tab. This will prompt the pop-up menu to open.
3. Select the **Monetization** tab on the left-hand side of the menu.
4. Now, enable private servers by clicking on the green toggle button. This will also create a larger dropdown containing more parameter options.
5. By default, private servers are set to free. To change this, select the **Paid** option underneath in the expanded **Options** menu.
6. Next, set the price for the servers.

    Remember that the subscription is renewed monthly, so if you set the price to 100 Robux, you will earn 100 Robux per server every month unless they cancel it.
7. Select the **Save** button at the bottom of the menu to overwrite the existing options.

And with that, you now know the quickest way to set up private servers for your experience. For more information as to why private servers are important to utilize, see the *There's more...* section of this recipe.

There's more...

Why are private servers so popular? There are many reasons, such as having the ability to explore and roam a game without other players in your server getting in your way. This is because one of the main perks of having a private server is that you can customize who is allowed to enter – if anyone. This makes it easier for content creators to stream and record videos, which inherently boosts your game's exposure. Other players like to be in private servers to grind experience points without people around. No matter the reason, private servers are a very popular commodity.

Engagement-based payouts

Roblox offers something to developers called **premium payouts**. This is a way to reward you with Robux for retaining players who have Roblox Premium in your experience for long periods of time. A good way to do this is by offering premium players some sort of perk or access to an otherwise locked location.

In this recipe, we will look at the steps to creating a premium-only door as well as how to create a sign using **SurfaceGui** and **TextLabel** objects. Let's examine how.

How to do it...

We will start by creating a simple door using a square part. Next, we will change the name and transparency of the door part. We will then add an invisible part overtop of the doorway. Then, we will insert **SurfaceGui** and **TextLabel** objects and modify their parameters to give us our desired style of text. To start, follow these steps:

1. Insert a square part into **Workspace** and scale it to the size of the entrance of the room you would like to make accessible to premium members only. In this example, my door is `12 x 10 x 1` studs large.
2. Rename the door part `PremiumDoor`.
3. Change the **PremiumDoor** part's **Transparency** value to `0.6`. This will allow players to look in and get a glimpse of the cool things inside, drawing them toward the door.
4. Next, insert a second part to use as a sign above the door.
5. Rename the part `TextSign`.
6. Change the **TextSign** part's **Transparency** value to `1`.
7. Right-click the part and insert a **SurfaceGui** object.
8. With the **SurfaceGui** object selected in the explorer window, set the **Face** property to the correct orientation if it is not already.
9. In the **Sizing** section of the property box, change the **SizingMode** property value to **PixelsPerStud**.
10. Set the **PixelsPerStud** value to about `40`. You may need to raise or lower this depending on the size and length of the text that you will insert.

11. Next, right-click the **SurfaceGui** object in the explorer and then insert **TextLabel**.
12. Select the **TextLabel** object and then select the **Text** textbox.
13. Write `PREMIUM ONLY` in the textbox.
14. Change the **TextColor3** value to a noticeable color. In this example, I'm using blue for my text color.
15. Enable the **TextScaled** property option.
16. Increase the **TextSize** value to fill the sign space.
17. Select the **FontFace** property to open a drop-down menu of available fonts.

    You can download more in **Toolbox** under the **Fonts** category in search.
18. You can bold your text and/or add italics to your text by clicking on their designated icons beside the **Style** property option.
19. Next, insert the `PremiumDoorScript` script found in the `Chapter 9` folder into **Workspace**.
20. Move the script from **Workspace** into the door part.

With that, you've successfully created a working premium-only door:

Figure 9.4: Completed premium-only door

If you were to place some cool items or create a unique social environment behind the door, it would attract the ones with premium to check it out.

This chapter has shown you not one, not two, but five different ways to generate Robux through your game or experience. We first examined the one-time payment option that gamepasses provide us and how we can reward the player with an exclusive item for owning the pass. We then created a tip jar using developer products that can be purchased multiple times. Next, we saw how to leverage paid access for the early stages of the game before launch, and then the benefits of having private servers. Lastly, we saw how Roblox provides developers with an opportunity to earn Robux through premium members playing our game, and how we can use the VIP door method to attract said members.

10
Extra Building Recipes

This chapter will focus on a few extra recipes that will help heighten the quality of your experience. Using some preset weapons, vehicles, and emote bars, you will learn how to customize their sound, damage, speed, particle, beam effects, and many other parameters, which will help ensure the item is a proper fit for your needs. We will also look at how we can enable multi-person team creation, as well as a step-by-step walk-through of the **Game Settings** tab. Let's jump into it!

In this chapter, we will be looking at six different recipes that you can include in your experiences:

- Modifying a weapon system
- Swords as tools
- Vehicle system basics
- Building a custom emote bar
- Enabling **Team Create**
- Customizing your game settings

Technical requirements

For this chapter, you will need to open your experience with the latest version of Roblox Studio. You will also need to use the assets provided within the `Chapter 10` folder available at https://packt.link/gbz/9781805121596, which include the necessary **weapon**, **vehicle**, and **emote bar** systems.

Modifying a weapon system

Roblox has provided us with a large library of items and tools that we can use and modify. One of the provided items that we will be examining in this recipe is weapons, specifically guns. We will examine how to best configure the various weapon **IntValues** (*store integers*), such as ammo capacity and hit damage. To finish, we will work to modify the audio and visual appearance of the weapon.

How to do it...

We will begin by inserting a weapon into the **StarterPack** object, and then move the **WeaponsSystem** script into the **ServerScriptService** object. Next, we will open the `Configuration` folder and modify various parameters such as **AmmoCapacity** and **HitDamage**. Next, we will apply a new texture onto the gun model; then we will change the **SoundID** property value, followed by changing the **ColorSequence** and **Width** values of the muzzle flash particle effect. To begin, follow these steps:

1. To begin, download the **Weapons Kit** model for **Auto Rifles** from **Creator Marketplace**, or in **Toolbox | See All | WEAPONS**.

2. In this example, I am using an **Assault Rifle** (**AR**).

    Alternatively, you can find weapons by going to **Toolbox | See All | Weapons**.

3. Open Roblox Studio and insert the **Auto Rifles** kit from the **Weapons** section of the toolbox.

4. Select **Yes** when asked to add the tools to **Starterpack**. Items inside **StarterPack** will be copied into the player's backpack when they spawn, so they are able to equip the tool.

5. Move the `WeaponsSystem` folder found inside one of the weapons into the **ServerScriptService** object. The `WeaponsSystem` script will allow us to modify all of the main weapon settings.

6. Now, delete the **WeaponsSystem** script from all other weapons as it's not needed.

7. Under the gun that you wish to set up, open the `Configuration` folder dropdown located inside the gun model. This gives us a large selection of items that we can customize, mostly through adjusting number values. In this recipe, I will be working with the **AR2** model.

8. Select the **AmmoCapacity IntValue** object and then change the number inside the value box to `45`. This is how much ammo will be stored in each magazine.

9. Next, select the **HitDamage IntValue** object and change it to `20`. This is the amount of damage done by every bullet.

10. Moving onto **MaxSpread**, set the value to `0.5`. The smaller the number, the tighter the spread pattern, meaning it will be more accurate.

11. Next, change the **RecoilMax** value to `0.75`.

12. Change the value of **RecoilMin** to `0.6`.

13. Now, set the **TotalRecoilMax** value to `0.9`.

14. Now, to apply a new texture to the model, copy and paste the **AR2** model from the **StarterPack** object into **Workspace**, and then press *F* on your keyboard to bring the model into your camera's frame. This will help us visualize the changes that we will make to the texture.

15. Inside the gun model, select the part named **Rifle**. Unlike regular Roblox parts, this gun model is broken up into three meshparts. Meshparts are `Obj`- or `Fbx`-formatted models that were created and then imported into Roblox from third-party software such as Blender or Maya.

16. To change the meshpart's color and material, we will be changing the texture UV map to a new one:

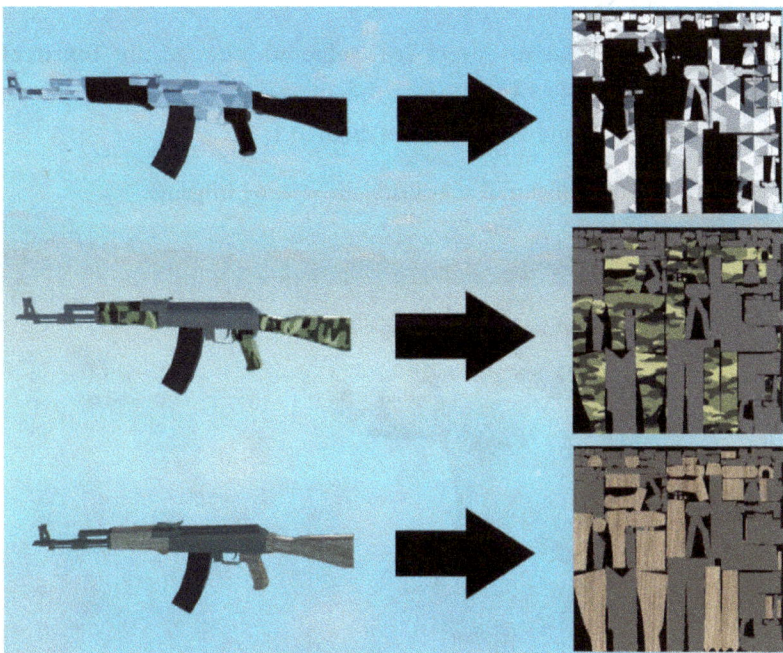

Figure 10.1: Texture UVs

UV maps allow us to apply 2D textures onto the 3D meshpart and have it wrap to fit the model. You can try some of the following texture IDs for yourself:

- rbxassetid://15300805629
- rbxassetid://15300790365
- rbxassetid://15300948698
- rbxassetid://15300793551

17. Next, we will change the gun firing sound. To do so, select the **Fired** sound object inside of the **Rifle MeshPart** dropdown.

18. Change the **SoundID** value to one of the following:

- 4314625021
- 2811598570
- 1905367471

19. Next, to change the **Color** value of the flash that comes out of the barrel when we shoot, select the **MuzzleFlash Beam** object, and then change its **ColorSequence** value to `197, 154, 0` and `255, 196, 0`.
20. With the **MuzzleFlash Beam** object still selected, change the **TextureID** value to `rbxassetid://872910628`.
21. Finally, change the **Width0** and **Width1** values, both to `1.2`.

Figure 10.1 shows we can use the bullet trail after firing the weapon in-game:

Figure 10.2: Modified weapon system

You now have a solid understanding of how to modify the various aspects of the weapon, such as customizable **IntValue** objects, sound, and muzzle flash beams. Let's now move on to see how we can customize gears in the next recipe.

Swords as tools

Tools are a type of object that a humanoid (player) can equip from their **Backpack**. Any tool that we wish for players to start and respawn with should be placed inside of the **StarterPack** object. Once set up properly, this will allow players to select numbers on their keyboard or by clicking the **Tools** icon on the screen if they're on mobile. Let's look at how we can set up and modify the various aspects of a Roblox sword tool.

How to do it...

We will first locate and then insert the **SwordOfLight** model into the **StarterPack** object. This model can be found here: `roblox.com/library/14971508851`. We will then delete the **ThumbnailCamera** object and customize the **PointLight** color. Next, we will change the **Lunge** and **Unsheath SoundID** values and then change the **RollOffMaxDistance** and **Volume** values. Then, we will modify the flare **ParticleEmitter** object and then modify the server script to give the sword a different property value. Finally, we will change the sword **TextureID** value. All the code for this recipe is provided inside of the sword model.

> **Important note**
> All the *line numbers* listed in the steps of this recipe can be found in the code for the sword model.

To start, follow these steps:

1. Insert the **SwordOfLight** model into the player's **StarterPack** object. The **StarterPack** object is where users' equipable inventory items are stored. You can find the **SwordOfLight** model inside **Toolbox | See All | WEAPONS**.
2. Now, move the **SwordOfLight** model to inside the **StarterPack** object.
3. In the **Properties** box under the **Behavior** tab, disable **CanBeDropped**. This will disallow players from dropping their sword on the ground, forcing it to remain in their starter pack.
4. Delete the **ThumbnailCamera** object inside of the sword model.
5. Now, open the **Handle** dropdown inside of the sword model.
6. Now, select the **PointLight** object and change its **Color** to orange (`255, 132, 128`).
7. Next, select the **Lunge** sound object found under the same **Handle** dropdown.
8. Change the **SoundID** value to one of the following:
    - `3052201463`
    - `9119750538`
    - `9119751891`
9. Change the **RollOffMaxDistance** value to `7000`. This will affect the maximum distance (in studs) that a client's listener can hear audio being emitted from the object.
10. Set the **Volume** value to `0.45`.
11. Now, select the **Unsheath** sound object found under the **Handle** dropdown.

12. Change the **SoundID** value to one of the following:

    - 9119742469
    - 9119742466
    - 9119747270

13. Next, select the **ParticleEmitter** object named **Flare** found under the **Effects** attachment in the **Handle** dropdown.

14. Change the **<ColorSequence>** value to fade from yellow (`248, 237, 122`) to orange (`255, 132, 128`).

15. Next, change the **Speed** value to `6`.

16. Change the **Rate** value to `24`.

17. Now, to modify the sword's properties, double-click the script titled **Server** to open the script editor.

18. On *line 37* (`Damage = 14`), change the **Damage** number value to `6`. This is the default damage that is given when someone touches the blade.

19. Now, on *line 39* (`SpecialReload = 30`), change the number to `20`. This number is how many seconds it takes for the sword's special ability to reload.

    You can test the abilities of the sword by clicking *Q* and *E* on your keyboard while in **Play** mode.

20. Next, to change the logo that appears on the ground during our special attack, select **Circle**, found inside of **SwordOfLight** | **Server** | **TimeChange** | **CelestialCircle** | **Circle**.

21. Insert the **TextureID** value that you would like to use, or use one of the following:

    - rbxassetid://15301153515
    - rbxassetid://15301172447
    - rbxassetid://15301155445

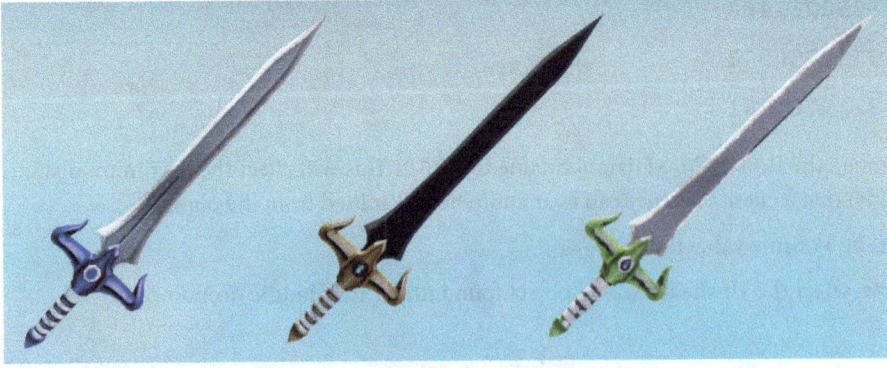

Figure 10.3: Textured swords

22. Next, select the **ParticleEmitter** object named **Stars**, found under the **TimeChange** script dropdown.
23. Insert a custom **TextureID** value or use one of the following:

    - 10002492897
    - 11815755770
    - 7924475318

24. Now, change the **Color** value of the star particles. In this example, I used the 109, 218, 248 color.
25. Next, enable **LightInfluence** in the top **Appearance** tab.
26. Now, to change the sound of the special attack, select the sound object named **Strike** inside of the same **TimeChange** script.
27. Change the **SoundID** value to one of the following:

    - 2789419376
    - 3406813517
    - 689589276

28. Finally, select the **SwordMesh** object inside of the **Handle** dropdown and then insert one of the following **TextureID** values to change the visual appearance of the sword's texture:

    - 14959745277
    - 14959745832
    - 14959746388

In *Figure 10.4*, we can see the final result of our sword customization:

Figure 10.4: Sword tool

As you can see through completing these steps, you don't need to be a savant of coding in order to thoroughly modify various elements of gear. We were able to change not only the damage and ability recharge time, but also the sounds, particles, beams, point lights, and even the sword texture itself.

There's more...

If you want to change the sword mesh entirely while still maintaining the functionality, you can change the **MeshID** value inside **SwordMesh**. You may need to modify the **Scale** and **Offset** values found in the property box to position it correctly in the player's hand. Here are a few fun examples of different sword meshes you can try out by inserting the following IDs into the handle's **MeshID** value:

- 409664704
- 4613928725
- 437948651

Vehicle system basics

In this recipe, we will be adjusting various elements of the preset vehicle template such as its sounds, speed, and texture. The recipe will also demonstrate how to modify parameters both by modifying the vehicle's scripts and then the easier way to set it up through modifying the **NumberValues** configuration.

How to do it...

We will start by inserting the vehicle into **Workspace** and then open the **Chassis** script where we will modify the **MaxSpeed**, **ReverseSpeed**, **Gravity**, **DrivingTorque**, and **BrakingTorque** values. We will then change the ignition time found inside the **Effects** script, and then enable **CarJacking** in the **VehicleSeating** script. We will then modify the sounds followed by changing the remaining parameters through the **Customization** dropdown, and then finish the vehicle by customizing the textures and appearance. All the code for this recipe is provided inside of the vehicle model.

> **Important note**
> All the *line numbers* listed in the steps of this recipe can be found in the code for the vehicle model.

Let's see how:

1. To begin, open Roblox Studio to a blank baseplate.
2. Insert the vehicle found in the `Chapter 10` folder.
3. Select the vehicle in the Explorer and then open its **Scripts** folder.
4. Double-click the **Chassis** script to open the script editor.

5. Change the number value of the **MaxSpeed** object on *line 20* (`MaxSpeed = 75/mphConversion`) to `85`, or whatever you desire the maximum speed that the vehicle can travel.
6. Likewise, adjust the number value of **ReverseSpeed** on *line 21*. In this example, it is set to `48`.
7. On *line 51*, you can choose to modify the gravity of the car. By default, it is set to `196.2`. The higher the number, the heavier the gravity, and the lower the number, the lower the gravity. In this example, I will leave the number at its default.
8. Increase the **DrivingTorque** value to `32000` on *line 23*. This will allow our vehicle to climb up steep slopes with more ease.
9. Set the **BrakingTorque** value to `72000` to increase the stopping ability of the vehicle.
10. Next, open the **Effects** script inside the `Scripts` folder.
11. On *line 17*, change the **IgnitionTime** value to `1.25` seconds. The higher the number, the longer it takes to start the vehicle.
12. Now, open the **VehicleSeating** script.
13. On *line 6*, enter the number of seconds that you want it to take for someone to open the vehicle door. In this example, it's set to `1`.
14. If you wish to allow carjacking (other players can steal your car), then replace `false` with `true` on *line 20*.
15. Now that we are a little more familiar with the customizable code, navigate to the `Configuration` folder and open it.
16. Select **MaxEngineRPM** and then change the value to `6000`. Similarly, you can modify the number value of any of these configuration options to quickly tune the vehicle.
17. Now, to modify the vehicle sounds, open the `Effects` folder dropdown.
18. Select **EngineStart** and then navigate to the **Properties** box.
19. Change the **SoundID** value of **Idle** to one of the following:
    - 912961304
    - 836996297
    - 8166922677
20. Change the **SoundID** value of **OpenCloseDoor** to `5349327087`.
21. Next, we will modify the graphics on the vehicle body by first selecting the **Hood** mesh in the model.
22. Select the hood, `LF_door`, `LR_door`, `RF_door`, `RR_door`, `RR_fender`, `LR_fender`, and `rear_fender` meshparts.

23. Change the meshpart's **Texture** value to one of the following:

    - `rbxassetid://5191006921`
    - `rbxassetid://9218594709`
    - `rbxassetid://32506484`

Figure 10.5: Vehicle texture variants

24. Now, we will place a decal onto an unanchored square part and place it on the side of the vehicle. A decal is an image that takes the shape of the surface it's applied to. Unlike textures, you cannot change the offset or **StudsPerTile** with decals.
25. Move the part with the decal applied to it into the vehicle model.
26. Select the vehicle model, and then select **Weld** from the constraint's **Create** dropdown menu inside the **Model** tab of the top bar. Welding the parts together will keep the unanchored decal from falling off of the vehicle.
27. Next, click on both the decal part and the meshpart that it is applied to on the vehicle. This will weld the two parts together.
28. Now, we will continue to customize the vehicle's appearance by selecting the meshpart called **Glass**.
29. Change the **Transparency** value to `.6`.
30. Change the **Reflectance** value to `0.6`.
31. Change the glass **Color** value to `35, 61, 54`.
32. Next, we will adjust the distance it takes for the enter car prompt attached to the chassis to become visible to the player. We will then go to the drop-down menu of **SeatFR**, and open the dropdown to **PromptLocation**. We will then select **EndorsedVehicleProximityPromptV1**.
33. In the property box, set the **KeyboardKeyCode** value to whichever key you want players to press to enter. Usually, it's best to keep it at *E*.

34. Set the **MaxActivationDistance** value to `15`. The higher the number, the farther away someone can get in from.

35. Change the **ObjectText** name to whatever the vehicle's name is, or what you want it to say when players get close.

36. Finally, change the value of **HoldDuration** to `0.25`. The higher the number, the longer someone must hold the button that we set in *step 33* to enter the vehicle.

In *Figure 10.6*, we can see the finished vehicle in action:

Figure 10.6: Vehicle system

Through this recipe, you have successfully modified the chassis script to change different values for torque and speed, changed the sounds and appearance of the car, and even enabled carjacking. Now, you have a general outline for how you can modify the toolbox's provided **Cars** system.

Building a custom emote bar

A great way to encourage socialization and organic interactions within your experience is by including an emote bar. Roblox provides us with a built-in dev module, which we will be exploring in this recipe. By the end of this recipe, you will have a fully functioning emote bar filled with your desired emotes.

How to do it…

We will start by inserting the **Emote Bar** model, which can be found here: `roblox.com/library/14971586392`. Next, we will place it into the **ServerScriptService** object and then open the **ConfigureEmotes** script. Here, we will copy and paste a chunk of code multiple times, and then go through and number each chunk sequentially. Next, we will navigate to the catalog where we will find and copy emote IDs that we will paste inside of the **AnimationIDGrabber** script and run to get the **AnimationID** value. We will then paste the **AnimationID** value into the script and then modify the name and image of the emote. All the code for this recipe is provided inside of the `Emote Bar` folder.

184 Extra Building Recipes

> **Important note**
> All the *line numbers* listed in the steps of this recipe can be found in the code for the **Emote Bar** model.

To begin, follow these steps:

1. Open up Roblox Studio to a blank baseplate.
2. Insert the **Emote Bar** file found inside the `Chapter 10` folder or locate it in **Toolbox | Models | See All | Dev Modules**. This shows you all available free-to-use developer modules.
3. Now, drag the **EmoteBar** model from **Workspace** into the **ServerScriptService** object found in the Explorer window. When you playtest, an emote bar should come up with a few emojis along the bottom of your screen:

Figure 10.7: Emote bar

4. Next, drag the **ConfigureEmotes** script from **Workspace** into the **ServerScriptService** object.
5. Open the **ConfigureEmotes** script.
6. On *line 6*, change the script from `true` to `false`.
7. Now, to add more emotes, copy *lines 10* to *15* of the script:

    ```
    {
    name = "Cheer",
    animation = "rbxassetid://5895324424",
    image = "rbxassetid://12422929849",
    defaultTempo = 1,
    },
    ```

8. Next, paste the copied code underneath the original. Repeat this step until you have your desired amount of emotes.
9. Now, correct the number order sequence shown at the bottom of each string beside **defaultTempo**. For example, **defaultTempo** on *line 14* should be 1, **defaultTempo** on *line 20* should be 2, **defaultTempo** on *line 26* should be 3, and so on.
10. Next, to find emotes to use, navigate to the Roblox web page and go to the **Marketplace** section.
11. In the **Item Sort** dropdown beside the search bar, select **Animations**.

12. Find an animation from a catalog that you want to use and then open it in a new tab in your browser. In this example, I'm using the **Applaud** emote.
13. Copy the **number ID** value in the URL of the emote. In this example, the ID for the applaud emote is 5915779043. This is the **number ID** value.
14. To get the animation ID, go back to Studio and then insert a new script into **Workspace** or insert the **AnimationIDGrabber** script located inside of the Chapter 10 folder.
15. Insert the following code into the blank script:

    ```
    local id = game.InsertService:LoadAsset(999999)
    id.Parent = game.ReplicatedStorage
    ```

16. Paste the **number ID** value that you copied in *step 13* and paste it in place of 999999 in the script.
17. Now, run the game by navigating to the **Test** tab in the top bar, clicking the drop-down arrow of the **Play** button, and then selecting **Run**.
18. With the game running, open the model that contains the script created inside of the **ReplicatedStorage** object and select the child of the model, which should have the same name as the animation.
19. In the property box, copy the number string inside of the **AnimationID** box.
20. Now, in the **ConfigureEmotes** script, paste the = rbxassetid:// **AnimationID** value at the end of the second animation, which should be on *line 18* of the script.
21. Change the name of the emote on *line 17* to the name of your animation. In this example, I changed it to Applaud.
22. Now, go back to the baseplate in Roblox Studio and insert a square part.
23. Insert a **Decal** object onto one of the surfaces of the square.
24. Upload the image from your file explorer that you would like to use for the emote icon. Alternatively, there are several icons that can be used in the Chapter 10 folder.
25. Once your image is uploaded onto the part, copy the rbxassetid value inside of the texture field box in the properties.
26. Open the **ConfigureEmotes** script and paste the **rbxassetid** value in place of the existing **rbxassetid** value on *line 19* of the script.
27. Now, repeat *steps 11-25* until you have filled the script with your new emote animations.
28. To test your emote bar, click **Play** in the **Test** tab in the top bar of Studio. Clicking **1**, **2**, **3**, and so on should cause your avatar to emote:

Figure 10.8: Emote bar

Enabling Team Create

Roblox allows you to enable **Team Create**, which enables you to add your friends to a list of individuals with **Edit** permission. This allows multiple people to have access to and edit studio at the same time. It also is beneficial to enable **Team Create** even when working alone in Studio because it has both autosaving as well as script version control. Enabling it is straightforward, so let's get ready and look at the steps.

How to do it...

First, we will open the **Team Create** window by selecting **Team Create** in the **View** tab. We will then turn on the **Team Create** button, which will refresh our studio. We will then set our parameters and invite our friends to **Team Create**. To begin the recipe, follow these steps:

1. First, open up Roblox Studio to an empty baseplate, or to the game that you wish to enable **Team Create** on.
2. Navigate to the **View** tab found in the top bar of Studio.
3. Select **Team Create** to open the **Team Create** window.
4. In the newly opened window, click the **Turn On** button to enable **Team Create**. If the place is not published to Roblox, then it will instead say **Save to Roblox**, in which case you must save the place first.
5. Once you have clicked the button, it should refresh Studio. Once Studio has been refreshed, select **Collaborate** at the top-right corner of Studio.
6. Now, once clicked, a pop-up menu will open. Type in the name of the user or group you would like to grant access to.
7. Select the dropdown beside the user that you added.

8. Select either **Play** or **Edit**.
9. **Play** allows them to play the experience, and **Edit** will allow them Studio access. Note that only friends can be granted **Edit** access.
10. Select **Save** at the bottom of the popup.

This concludes the steps for setting up **Team Create** in your place. Check out the *There's more...* section of this recipe for a second method to enable **Team Create** in new places.

There's more...

A second way to enable **Team Create** when starting in a new unpublished place is to enable the **Team Create** button at the bottom of the **Publish Game** pop-up menu. This will then automatically turn on **Team Create** when it refreshes the place automatically when you select the **Create** button.

Customizing your game settings

In the final recipe of this chapter, we will examine how we can configure in-game communication, access permissions, upload badges, and create developer products as well as modify world properties such as gravity, walk speed, and jump height through the **Game Settings** page. The steps will examine the various aspects of the **Game Settings** menu and see how we can apply it to our experience.

How to do it...

We will first open the **Game Settings** tab in Studio, and then go through the 10 different tabs one by one while examining the various options provided within each tab, starting with the **Basic Info** tab. To begin, follow these steps:

1. Open **File | Game Settings** or open game settings from the **Home** tab of the top toolbar of Studio. This will create a popup of the **Game Settings** menu.
2. On the left of the box, select the **Basic Info** tab. Here, you can adjust your game's **Name**, **Description**, **Icon**, **Thumbnail**, **Genre**, **Age Recommendation**, and **Playable Devices** values.
3. Next, select the **Communication** tab. You can enable **Voice chat** by turning on the **Enable Microphone** button. Turn on the **Enable Camera** option to allow camera tracking for avatar animations for those who have it enabled in their account settings.
4. Now, select the **Permissions** tab and then select one of the three choices:

    - **Friends** allows only your friends on Roblox to join the experience
    - **Public** allows anyone to join
    - **Private** allows only the developers to join the experience

5. Moving to the **Monetization** tab now, you can upload badges and developer products from here as well as enable **Private Servers** and **Paid Access**.

6. Next, select the **Security** tab. Here, you can select these options:

    - **Allow HTTP Requests**
    - **Third Party Sales**
    - **Teleports**
    - **Enable Studio Access to API Services**

    It's not recommended that you enable these unless you're aware of what you're doing.

7. Moving onto the **Places** tab, here, you can create a sub-place within the main experience.

8. In the **Localization** tab, you can set up the game's **Source Language** type as well as set up **Automatic Translation** in various languages.

9. Now, select the **Avatar** tab. Here, you can choose the experience's default **Avatar Preset** objects such as the type of avatar, animation, and collisions. You can also set the **Scale** value for player height and proportions, and even override players' body parts and clothing all together.

10. In the **World** tab now, Roblox provides us with three presets with varying settings: **Classic**, **Realistic**, and **Action**. Alternatively, you can enter your own parameters in each field's box. You can modify the world **Gravity**, **Jump Height**, and **Power** values, the player's **Walkspeed** value, and the **Max Slope Angle** value at which players can walk up.

11. Lastly, we will look at the **Other** tab. Here, you can select **Enable Collaborative Editing**, which allows people within **Team Create** to edit scripts together simultaneously. You are also able to choose **Shutdown All Servers** in case, for whatever reason, you need to force a game-wide shutdown. Now, when another user joins **Team Create**, you will see a hovering circle with their username above it.

    With that final walk-through step, you should now have a clear understanding of how to quickly modify a multitude of settings within this single settings box.

This chapter has given you the final bit of knowledge that you need to successfully create and launch your own experience. You have learned how to modify the many parameters found within these tools and systems, first by adjusting the values within the tools' scripts, and secondly, by configuring the **IntValue** objects laid out for us. You've learned how to add onto and customize an emote bar, as well as how to enable **Team Create**. And finally, we saw how we can modify all our experience settings through the **Game Settings** menu.

With this concluding the final chapter of the *Roblox Cookbook*, I thank you for reading it and hope that you found the steps easy to follow and helpful for building your Roblox career.

Until next time, happy building, and remember... don't forget to anchor your parts!

Index

Symbols

3Dtext Generator plugin 99, 100

A

Animated Textures 77
arch
  unioning 34-36
Archimedes plugin 88, 90, 92
Assault Rifle (AR) 174

B

Beam object
  using, to create laser 75, 76
bed
  building 16-20
biomes 42
  generating 42, 43
broken wall
  creating 36-38

C

cactuses
  building 4-6

cereal bowl
  modeling 29-31
chair
  creating 2-4
Constructive Solid Geometry (CSG) tools 25
custom emote bar
  building 183-185

D

desert landscape
  creating 55, 56
details, on surfaces
  engraving 31-34
developer products
  using 166-168

E

engagement-based payouts 170
erupted volcano
  sculpting 61-65

F

fire effects
  creating 68-70

Index

first-time user experience (FTUE) 123
Flipbook textures 77, 78
functional TV
   building 9-12

G

gamepasses 163
   creating 164-166
game settings
   customizing 187, 188
grayboxing 112, 115

H

hand-sculpted hills
   creating 49-51
hand-sculpting 49
heightmap 46
   terrain, stamping with 46
hi-res fire
   creating, with particle effects 71-73
holes
   carving 26-29
house
   blueprinting 104, 105
   ceilings, adding 115-117
   doors, adding 110
   finalizing 119-122
   floors, adding 109, 110
   lights, adding 116, 117
   props, grayboxing 112-114
   roof and front overhang, creating 117-119
   walls, building 105-108
   windows, adding 111

I

intersecting 40
island
   creating 52-54

L

ladder
   creating 12-15
laser
   creating, with Beam object 75, 76
low-poly rocks
   sculpting, from block 39, 40

M

mountain, with waterfall
   creating 57-59
multiplayer obby game
   lava bricks, creating 95, 96
   lobby, building 88-90
   path of trusses, creating 94
   respawn checkpoints, setting up 100, 101
   slide, creating 92, 93
   spinning blades 96-98
   template, designing 90, 91
   winners' area, building 99, 100
Multiple Part Resizer plugin 89, 94

N

Negate function 26
negating 40
non-player character (NPC) 132

Index

P

paid access
  setting up 168
  using 168
part 1
particle effects
  used, for creating hi-res fire 71-73
  used, for making volumetric smoke 73, 74
ParticleEmitter object
  using 84, 85
premium-only door
  creating 170, 171
premium payouts 170
private servers 169
  enabling 169, 170
  prices, setting 169
PvP map
  finishing 160, 161
  grayboxing 148-152
  layout, planning 144-147
  outer perimeter, creating 156, 157
  props, placing for cover 154, 155
  risk, versus reward spots 152-154
  volumetric lighting, adding 158, 159

R

Resize Align plugin 88, 90, 93, 100, 119

S

shingling 1
single-player map
  ambient sounds, adding 141, 142
  atmosphere, creating with lighting 138-140
  building out 135-138
  flow 123
  locked door, creating 130-132
  obstacles, adding 132-134
  planning 124-127
  player forward, drawing 127-129
smoke effects
  creating 68-70
sparkles effects
  creating 68-70
stone water well
  creating 20-24
sword tool 176-179

T

Team Create
  enabling 186, 187
terrain
  landscapes, creating from scratch 43-46
  properties, modifying 47, 48
  stamping, with heightmap 46, 47
ThreeDtext Generator
  plugin 88, 89, 104, 105
Trail effect 79
  implementing 79-81
trusses 94

U

Union function 26
unioning 40

V

vehicle system basics 180-182
visual effects (VFX) 67
volumetric smoke
  making, with particle effects 73, 74
Voxel Terrain 41

W

weapon system
 modifying 173-176
whirlwind
 building 82, 83
wooden crates
 creating 7-9

Z

Z-clipping 9
Z-fighting 9

www.packtpub.com

Subscribe to our online digital library for full access to over 7,000 books and videos, as well as industry leading tools to help you plan your personal development and advance your career. For more information, please visit our website.

Why subscribe?

- Spend less time learning and more time coding with practical eBooks and Videos from over 4,000 industry professionals
- Improve your learning with Skill Plans built especially for you
- Get a free eBook or video every month
- Fully searchable for easy access to vital information
- Copy and paste, print, and bookmark content

Did you know that Packt offers eBook versions of every book published, with PDF and ePub files available? You can upgrade to the eBook version at packtpub.com and as a print book customer, you are entitled to a discount on the eBook copy. Get in touch with us at customercare@packtpub.com for more details.

At www.packtpub.com, you can also read a collection of free technical articles, sign up for a range of free newsletters, and receive exclusive discounts and offers on Packt books and eBooks.

Other Books You May Enjoy

If you enjoyed this book, you may be interested in these other books by Packt:

Mastering Roblox Coding

Mark Kiepe

ISBN: 978-1-80181-404-1

- Understand and learn the basics of Roblox Luau
- Discover how to write efficient and optimized Luau code to avoid bad smells
- Explore how to optimize your game for PC, consoles, phones, and tablets
- Get up to speed with how to build databases using Luau
- Understand client and server functionalities and learn how to securely establish communication
- Discover how to build an advanced Roblox game from scratch

Coding Roblox Games Made Easy, Second Edition

Zander Brumbaugh

ISBN: 978-1-80323-467-0

- Use Roblox Studio and other free resources
- Learn coding in Luau: basics, game systems, physics manipulation, etc
- Test, evaluate, and redesign to create bug-free and engaging games
- Use Roblox programming and rewards to make your first game
- Move from lobby to battleground, build avatars, locate weapons to fight
- Character selection, countdown timers, locate escape items, assign rewards
- Master the 3 Ms: Mechanics, Monetization, Marketing (and Metaverse)
- 50 cool things to do in Roblox

Packt is searching for authors like you

If you're interested in becoming an author for Packt, please visit `authors.packtpub.com` and apply today. We have worked with thousands of developers and tech professionals, just like you, to help them share their insight with the global tech community. You can make a general application, apply for a specific hot topic that we are recruiting an author for, or submit your own idea.

Hi!

I'm Taylor Field-Draper, the author of The Ultimate Roblox Game Building Cookbook. I really hope you enjoyed reading this book and found it useful for increasing your productivity and efficiency in Roblox Game Building.

It would really help us (and other potential readers!) if you could leave a review on Amazon sharing your thoughts on The Ultimate Roblox Game Building Cookbook here.

Go to the link below or scan the QR code to leave your review:

`https://packt.link/r/1805121596`

Your review will help me to understand what's worked well in this book, and what could be improved upon for future editions, so it really is appreciated.

Best Wishes,

Taylor Field-Draper

Download a free PDF copy of this book

Thanks for purchasing this book!

Do you like to read on the go but are unable to carry your print books everywhere?

Is your eBook purchase not compatible with the device of your choice?

Don't worry, now with every Packt book you get a DRM-free PDF version of that book at no cost.

Read anywhere, any place, on any device. Search, copy, and paste code from your favorite technical books directly into your application.

The perks don't stop there, you can get exclusive access to discounts, newsletters, and great free content in your inbox daily

Follow these simple steps to get the benefits:

1. Scan the QR code or visit the link below

https://packt.link/free-ebook/9781805121596

2. Submit your proof of purchase
3. That's it! We'll send your free PDF and other benefits to your email directly

www.ingramcontent.com/pod-product-compliance
Lightning Source LLC
Chambersburg PA
CBHW080412170426
43194CB00015B/2785